(17)

204

Venezuela

1

‡‡‡‡‡‡‡‡‡‡‡‡‡ *National Planning Series* ‡‡‡‡‡‡‡‡‡‡‡‡

BERTRAM M. GROSS, GENERAL EDITOR

‡‡

JOHN FRIEDMANN is presently Director of the Ford Foundation Program of Urban and Regional Development in Chile. Prior to assuming this post he was Associate Professor of Regional Planning at the Massachusetts Institute of Technology and has served as consultant to the Venezuelan Guayana Development Corporation and the Interamerican Development Bank. Mr. Friedmann is the author of *Regional Policy for Developing Areas,* co-author of *Regional Development and Planning. A Reader,* and has contributed to professional journals, including the *Journal of the American Institute of Planners, Comparative Studies in Society and History, Land Economics,* and *Papers of the Regional Science Association.*

Venezuela

From Doctrine to Dialogue

JOHN FRIEDMANN

Preface by

BERTRAM M. GROSS

SYRACUSE UNIVERSITY PRESS

First Edition 1965

ACKNOWLEDGMENT

This and other volumes in the National Planning
Series were initiated with the encouragement and
support of Stephen K. Bailey, Dean of the Maxwell
Graduate School of Citizenship and Public Affairs,
Syracuse University, and of his predecessor, Harlan
Cleveland. They have been made possible through
a grant from the Ford Foundation for cross-cultural
research by the Maxwell School. In the final edit-
ing of the manuscript valuable assistance was provided by James Gies.

BERTRAM M. GROSS

Manufactured in the United States of America

TO

Enrique Tejera Paris

✠✠

Acknowledgments

I am greatly indebted to Professor Bertram M. Gross, who originally aroused my curiosity in the study of national planning and whose wise counsel during all stages of my work was deeply appreciated.

To my Venezuelan friends special thanks are due for introducing a novice to the subtleties of national politics. I am particularly grateful to Jorge Ahumada, Luís Lander, Alfonso Ravard, Roberto Alamo Blanco, Alexander Ganz, Julio Cotler, José Agustín Silva-Michelena, Eduardo Neira, José Alberto Rivas, and Clemente Chirinos, who all gave freely of their valuable time.

The detailed comments of Héctor Hurtado, Frank Bonilla, Edwin Lieuwen, and Fred Levy were exceedingly helpful in giving the study its present form.

The research was supported by a grant from the Maxwell Graduate School of Citizenship and Public Affairs of Syracuse University. But neither the school nor anyone mentioned above is in any sense responsible for any part of the material presented or for the opinions expressed.

J. F.

Contents

‡‡

The "Drifting Cloud" of Guided Development

Any book about Latin America by a "gringo" is apt to be—and perhaps should be—eyed with suspicion by Latin Americans.

The Latin American oligarchs and military juntas suspect that the U.S.A. is using the Alliance for Progress to foment social reform. The revolutionary left suspects the "North American imperialists" of always being primed for military intervention on behalf of reaction. The progressive middle forces suspect the "colossus of the North" of trying, through an updated Monroe Doctrine, to keep Latin American countries within a well-behaved "sphere of influence." All three resent the condescending approach of many *Norteamericanos* toward *Latinoamericanos,* including the gringo penchant for reserving the word "American" to refer exclusively to one country on the two American continents.

In the field of national economic planning there is special reason for suspicion. Experts from the United States, mostly without experience in planning at home, are "quick on the draw" with planning advice to Latin Americans. Although slow to criticize their own government for trade policies that hold back Latin American development, they are particularly quick to criticize Latin Americans for their failures in development. The sting of these criticisms is not moderated by the growing realization that national economic planning in Latin America is more notable for glowing paper promises than for concrete performance.

But John Friedmann's challenging study of national planning in Venezuela is an exception. The story he presents is less one of failure than of success. He approaches the subject as one interested more in learning from the Venezuelans than advising them. He sees Venezuelan experience as an indigenous phenomenon with world-wide implications, not as a mere tail to the kite of U.S. aid.

Besides, although a U.S. citizen, Friedmann is far from a gringo. Born in Vienna, he came to the U.S.A. as a refugee. After receiving the first Ph.D. from Rexford Tugwell's interdisciplinary planning program at the University of Chicago, he entered a career that has taken him to many parts of the world. He has worked not only in Venezuela but also in Brazil, Chile, and South Korea. He is a cosmopolitan scholar; one of the growing band of true "citizens of the world." Apart from its uses to Latin Americans, his study can be particularly helpful to North Americans sincerely interested in learning how to approach Latin American phenomena without the unwitting condescension of unstated premises of North American superiority.

This is not to say that Friedmann has held himself aloof from all the currents of social conflict in Venezuela. In disassociating himself from the presumed moral neutrality of national planning, he has made perfectly clear his support of those people and groups trying to build a "developmental society" in Venezuela. In so doing he has clearly favored opportunities for the old oligarchs to find constructive roles in economic development. He has clearly favored democratic, pluralistic processes of achieving some of the great visions of social revolutionaries.

Nevertheless, Friedmann has made a major contribution to the scientific study of national economic planning, one that serves as a valuable extension of the path-breaking work by Albert O. Hirschman.[1] In a field previously dominated almost entirely by abstract ideology and technocratic econometrics, he has developed a number of fresh and stimulating approaches. In so doing he has not tried to give an encyclopedic picture of Venezuelan planning or even to tell all that he knows on the subject. We shall not find here a blow-by-blow report on the laborious process of building CORDI-PLAN, the little CORDIPLANS and the major development corporations. He has not analyzed the relation between this vital institution-building process and the tremendous socioeconomic struggles over

[1] Albert O. Hirschman, *The Strategy of Economic Development* (New Haven: Yale University Press, 1958); ed., *Latin American Issues* (New York: Twentieth Century Fund, 1961); and *Journeys Toward Progress* (New York: Twentieth Century Fund, 1963).

land reform and relations with foreign oil companies. He has not related the planning process to the facts on unemployment and other aspects of economic performance. All this awaits subsequent study.

The key to Friedmann's analysis is found in the concept of development planning as "dialogue" rather than doctrine and in the image of Venezuela's national plan as a "drifting cloud." To this must be added his views on the crisis origins of national planning, the dynamics of regional planning (Friedmann's main love), the less advertised social objectives that loom behind the economic goals, and the effect of international currents. Each of these ideas has considerable relevance in other countries as well. Each ties in with various broad multidisciplinary questions [2] and hypotheses [3] that Friedmann and I have often debated between ourselves and with the authors of other studies in this series.

Let us now take a brief look at these central ideas.

NATIONAL PLANNING AS DIALOGUE

Central omnipotence and central omniscience are the two most wide-spread myths of national economic planning. Under the former some central authority is supposed to issue orders to government agencies, private enterprises, and individuals. Under the latter these orders are allegedly based on the findings of econometricians on the optimal allocation of resources. The two together yield a rational plan which is flexibly adjusted through "feedback information" to changing environmental circumstances. They provide the foundations for the doctrines of national economic planning found in both old-fashioned Marxism and new-fangled econometrics. In

[2] Bertram M. Gross, "National Planning: Some Fundamental Questions," *American Behavioral Scientist* (Dec. 1964), 7–13. The research questions presented in this article were prepared by a committee headed by economist Peter J. D. Wiles at the July 1964 Minnowbrook conference on "Action under Development Plans." This conference, in which John Friedmann actively participated, was sponsored jointly by the Maxwell School and the Comparative Administration Group of the American Society for Public Administration.

[3] Bertram M. Gross, "The Great Vista: National Planning Research," *Information* (Quarterly Bulletin, International Social Science Council; June 1965), 7–20. The 20 propositions discussed in this article were prepared at the Minnowbrook conference by a committee headed by historian Robert J. Shafer.

Latin American these doctrines provide encouragement for persistent tendencies to—in Hirschman's words—"escape to a dream world of ever-new laws, perfectly designed institutions or scientifically calculated plans." [4]

As one reads through Friedmann's explanation of Venezuela's new planning law of 1958, it appears almost too perfectly designed. Its provisions for general staff services by CORDIPLAN, a planning system linked to ministries and territorial subdivisions, for linkage with an annual program budget, for consultation—all these appear almost too scientifically calculated.

But in the law's administration one finds the pluralistic concept of national planning as a continuing "dialogue" among divergent groups and interests. As a general staff for the president, CORDIPLAN does not limit itself to the narrow functions of advising the president or acting as his representative. Rather, it concentrates upon serving as "a mediator of conflicting interests" (p. 33), providing a meeting ground for government ministries hitherto operating in "ministerial secrecy" (p. 37), developing " 'a personal relationship among the planners' " (p. 37), and building "communication bridges to all major decision poles" (p. 39). The Venezuelan plan is not just another doctrine among the many doctrines in a country where ideology is still rampant. It is rather a framework within which different views—indeed, different doctrines—are debated. The plan is treated "not as an inviolable document, a bible, but as a temporary summing-up of current knowledge, expectations, and desirabilities" (p. 39). The planning process is a framework for mutual adjustment among political leaders, ministries, private enterprise, and regional coalitions. "The great virtues of planning have been its tolerance and patience. Potential opponents found themselves in a quandary, attacking an enemy that would recede at every charge" (pp. 39–40). Under these circumstances the Venezuelan plan—in Friedmann's pungent phrase—is "somewhat like a drifting cloud" (p. 39).

Can a drifting cloud really serve as a guide to economic development? Can it promote national purposefulness in preventing economic drift?

Friedmann's general analysis indicates an affirmative answer.

[4] Hirschman, *Latin American Issues,* p. 41.

CORDIPLAN's shifting strategy "was played from strength, not weakness" (p. 40). The source of this strength may be partly explained by Mary Follett's concept of "power with" as contrasted with "power over." [5] CORDIPLAN's power, while rooted in legal authority and presidential backing, does not depend upon formal authority or presidential support alone. It increases its power by building up centers of power outside CORDIPLAN and developing relations of reciprocal influence with these centers. More specifically, one may infer that the planning process had a greater influence on economic events than Friedmann seems willing to concede. The worsening of Venezuela's economic situation from 1958 to 1961 was mainly the result of the world-wide decline in the price of oil, Venezuela's major export. Yet if it had not been for the new planning system, it seems likely that economic conditions would have deteriorated far more than they did.

THE CRISIS ORIGINS OF NATIONAL PLANNING

In surveying the emergence of ambitious national economic planning in many countries, I have been struck by one common characteristic: namely, the perception of serious crisis on the part of both key elites and wide masses of the people. Thus in the United States of America the war-time crises of two world wars each ushered in periods of central economic control. The anticipation of post-war depression helped bring about the quasi-planning system embodied in the Employment Act of 1946. In the Soviet Union the first Five Year Plan for industrialization (1928–33) was a response to the political crises created by the rise of traders and peasants under NEP in a country supposedly based upon an industrial proletariat. In France, after the Second World War, Jean Monnet's planning efforts were a response to war-time devastation. In analyzing reform movements in Latin America, Hirschman has pointed out that "crisis may make it possible to take action against powerful groups which are normally well entrenched and invulnerable, (and) . . . may stimulate action and hence learning on a

[5] Mary Follett, "Power," in Henry C. Metcalf and Lyndall Urwisk, eds., *Dynamic Administration: The Collected Papers of Mary Follett* (New York: Harper, 1942).

problem on which insight has been low and for that very reason has
not been tackled as long as it was in a quiescent state." [6]

Friedmann's analysis provides further corroboration of this general hypothesis. In 1946, at the time of the first Betancourt government, "a genuine crisis situation did not exist in Venezuela, and reasons for urgent structural reforms were not widely perceived" (p. 7). But in 1958, after a bloody decade of dictatorship by Pérez Jiménez, "the breaking-point of sufferance was reached" (p. 8). The political crisis was exacerbated by the economic crisis sparked by declining oil prices. Moreover, "a decade of rapid economic growth—the gross national product had doubled—and ostentatious living by a few had raised expectations to unreasonable heights" (p. 27). All this led to a fundamental crisis of frustration. The crisis atmosphere was sustained by the flight of capital, rising unemployment, and growing urban slums. It was heightened by *fidelismo* in nearby Cuba and by domestic conflicts over land reform and control of foreign oil companies. It was prolonged by national planning itself, which raised and extended aspirations for higher standards of living, public services, and personal autonomy. Thus national planning, "intended as a crisis-relieving instrument" (p. 28), helped create the conditions for its own survival.

But perceived crisis alone is never a sufficient condition for the emergence of national economic planning. While Latin American countries have suffered scores of serious crises, effective national planning has come into being only occasionally. In Venezuela, also, there had been serious crises before 1958. The difference is that in the period from 1958 to 1965 there have been many key leaders in strategic positions—such as Presidents Betancourt and Leoni and planners Tejera Paris, Guerrero, and Hurtado—who proved capable of creative responses to crisis.

In discussing this subject, Friedmann has made an important distinction between functional rationality and intended, adaptive rationality. The former is the technical rationality that concentrates upon means-ends chains. For its practitioners, a "crisis should never have arisen; that it has is interpreted as a failure of planning, as the result of distorted, 'irrational' behavior" (p. 29). Intended, adaptive rationality, in contrast, is based on the premise that "crises always occur when there is rapid change and this, of course, is

[6] *Journeys Toward Progress*, p. 261.

precisely the condition of modern economic development." It consists of "successfully adaptive behavior to crisis situations." It must therefore "sacrifice comprehensiveness to the urgency of overcoming specific bottlenecks; . . . be more problem- than goal-oriented; . . . be piecemeal and fragmented rather than coordinative" (p. 29).

THE DYNAMICS OF REGIONALISM

In dealing directly with the issues of regional development, Friedmann has grasped the nettle that national planners diligently try to avoid. Although all economic development takes place at some location in space-time, economic analysis traditionally deals with huge economic abstractions that lack spatial dimensions. This divorce of national planning from space is accentuated by the disciplinary barriers between the economists active at the national level and the architects, sociologists, and engineers who are the experts in local and regional planning. It is interesting to note that even though Venezuela's planning law envisaged inclusion of regional planning in national planning, CORDIPLAN started out with many reservations on the subject. In fact, rather than initiating ventures in this field, it responded to the logic of natural events.

The logic of these events was obviously all-compelling. First of all, the major political support of the dominant party, Democratic Action, has been in the periphery rather than in Caracas. Second, land reform—a major program of the party—was an operation extending over wide geographical areas. To the extent that it might lead to increased productivity (and there are indications that it has done so in many cases), it would accentuate the desirability for nonagricultural employment in the same areas. Third, the massive Guayana Valley program, with its hydroelectric and steel installations, created an example looked upon longingly by people in other regions.

The logic of dealing with competing regional demands is not so clear. "Two contradictory allocation criteria," Friedmann points out, were included in the national plan. The first was equity, which gave priority to the more backward regions. The second was return on investment, which gave priority to the more advanced regions. His brief discussion reminds us of the three sets of contradictory criteria which Peter Wiles finds in the rationalization of industrial location decisions under communist planning in the Soviet Union: (1) regional autarchy vs. regional specialization, (2) minimization of transport vs. maximization of scale of enterprise, and (3) location near the consumer vs. location near the raw material. With these considerations largely negating each other, and with profitable return on investment sparingly used, "the most important of all Communist criterion by far is *local political pull*." [7] It is interesting to note that with CORDIPLAN also, according to Friedmann, it was "for the political process to decide on the best investment of allocation funds" (p. 65).

But the word "politics" need not ring down the curtain on rationality—at least not for those who practice adaptive rather than functional rationality. The growth of regional planning institutions results in a more thoroughgoing representation and articulation of a people's varied interests. This makes the political dialogue more meaningful, even if more noisy. It holds forth the promise of promoting greater political stability, itself a condition for healthy economic development. It augurs "a shift in state politics away from the traditional emphasis on personalities to more substantive issues of development" and a forward step in "that complex process frequently referred to as nation-building" (p. 67). "The presumed loss of functional rationality is probably a deception on the part of technicians who regard planning as an abstract process of maximizing goal achievement along a single dimension" (p. 68).

One might question Friedmann's speculation concerning the temporary nature of the regional planning phenomenon. In another generation, he suggests, "a more nearly complete politicoeconomic integration across the national territory" will be achieved. Yet Venezuela already has the highest proportion of urban population of any Latin American country. In another generation one may anticipate that the urban revolution—with ever greater disparities between the metropolitan capital and the rest of the country—will reach full flower. This will probably create new crises, political and economic, and give a new impetus to regional planning.

[7] P. J. D. Wiles, *The Political Economy of Communism* (Cambridge: Harvard University Press, 1962), pp. 150–152.

SOCIAL SYSTEM OBJECTIVES

Planning has functions that are (a) explicit, open, and manifest, and (b) implicit, hidden, and latent.

Many of the conscious objectives and unintended consequences, as well as many of the means required for goal formulation, implementation and evaluation, are usually political, cultural, social or biophysical rather than merely economic.

These are two of the twenty Minnowbrook propositions on the nature of national planning.[8] The reader will probably not be surprised to learn that Friedmann's preliminary findings on Venezuela, along with other studies in this series, were available to the drafters.

Let me now make a little more explicit a number of points that are "latent" in Friedmann's analysis. First of all, the planning process has probably helped strengthen not only the presidency but also the capacities of many ministries to engage in both separate and concerted action. This, it might be noted, has also been a major function of French planning, with which Venezuelan planning has much in common. Second, in helping create a development society, the planning dialogue has helped bring into being a more organized and differentiated society. It has contributed to the growing role of the private business community and of such organizations as Fedecámeras and Pro-Venezuela. It has promoted the further differentiation of the many social groups—"white collar and skilled service workers, small tradesmen and farmers, as well as elitist groups of professionals, intellectuals, industrialists, and university students" (p. 5)—often referred to as "middle classes." Third, it has done more than—in Friedmann's sanitized phrase— "improve the political process." It has helped the Democratic Action party win elections. If it had not done this, there would be little political basis for planning's continued existence and its contribution to economic development.

Finally, in helping reduce social conflict, the national planning dialogue has probably contributed to Venezuela's relatively peaceful handling of the explosive problems of land reform and foreign oil companies. Venezuela "has the only government in Latin America that has introduced serious land expropriation without violent

[8] Gross, "The Great Vista: National Planning Research."

upheaval." [9] While the farmers' union often threatened to take over the land if it were not expropriated, the detailed land reform program (which included the distribution of public land as well as that bought from large land holders) was worked out by a "nonpartisan commission representing prominent political figures and private individuals of all shades of opinion." [10] Although foreign oil companies are the single largest factor in Venezuela's revenues in foreign and domestic currency, the government has handled this problem without resort to expropriation. It has imposed high taxes on the profits of foreign oil companies and helped obtain excellent wages and working conditions for their employees. Through the Venezuelan Petroleum Corporation, it has entered the oil business itself. This move probably contributed to the creation of the Creole Petroleum Company, a subsidiary of Standard Oil of New Jersey's Venezuelan company, established to stimulate domestic investment in "new non-oil related enterprises." [11] One of the most interesting aspects of this situation is the government's domestic success in achieving a high degree of freedom from foreign control without capitulation to the forceful ideologies favoring nationalization of foreign oil companies. In this connection it might be noted that oil is still the major factor in "mobilizing external resources," the last in Friedmann's list of latent objectives. Here the problem is not primarily one of recapturing the profits of the oil companies. It is mainly winning larger markets for Venezuelan oil against the competition of Middle Eastern oil and the resistance of U.S. coal interests who see in Venezuela's heavy oils a threat to their domestic business in the heating of homes and other buildings. In this fiercely competitive process Venezuela has been able to use the help of the foreign oil companies associated primarily with Venezuela and the minor Venezuelan subsidiaries of the other companies.[12]

Let us not assume that these many "latent" objectives of Venezuelan planning were all unintended or unanticipated. It is unlikely that they were hidden from the view of Tejera Paris, Guerrero, or

[9] John P. Powelson, *Latin America: Today's Economic and Social Revolution* (New York: McGraw Hill, 1964), p. 60.

[10] Thomas F. Carroll, "The Land Reform Issue in Latin America," in Albert O. Hirschman, ed., *Latin American Issues*, p. 185.

[11] Powelson, pp. 92–93.

[12] *Ibid.*, pp. 146–155.

Hurtado. Rather, under conditions which required action toward many objectives, common sense required explicit emphasis upon economic development objectives. Indeed, Friedmann's analysis clearly suggests that greater public attention to these noneconomic objectives might have interfered with their attainment. Why this may be so is a question that deserves deeper study. It may well turn out that more explicit goal formulation concerning the noneconomic dimensions of a social system will await the development of social system models that can compete in rigor and dramatic clarity with the national income models of the economists.[13]

INTERNATIONAL CURRENTS

Of general significance also is Friedmann's discussion of international influence upon Venezuelan planning practices.

During the 1950's the Economic Commission for Latin America (ECLA) "succeeded in making operational a concept of national economic planning within a democratic framework" (p. 25). It trained many of Latin America's leading economists, Venezuelans among them, and prepared them for future positions of leadership. At a later date it distributed a planning document that, "to all appearances is a manifesto giving the clarion call for social revolution" (p. 25). Yet ECLA ideas were not accepted in Venezuela without major modification. As an ECLA activist, Tejera Paris "stressed the social context of planning; he toned down the role of programming as the construction of econometric models" and stressed the need for a " 'habit of collaboration in the elaboration of the plans' " (p. 26).

Puerto Rican experience was also helpful, particularly in developing a commitment to planned development on the part of the future president of Venezuela. "Puerto Rican planning and ECLA programming thus came together into a fruitful union" (p. 27). But here again there was no question of an automatic adoption in Venezuela of methods developed elsewhere. The major effect of Puerto Rican planning was probably to inspire Venezuelans to develop an approach which they felt to be—and was—distinctively

[13] At the same time we should not go so far in stressing the uses of clarity as to forget the virtues of vagueness. See "The uses and language of vagueness" in "The Matrix of Purposes," Bertram M. Gross, *The Managing of Organizations* (New York: Free Press, 1964), II, 497.

their own. Indeed, there is a world of difference between the technocratic, nonpolitical planning ideas promulgated by Rexford Tugwell as Governor of Puerto Rico and the more pragmatic concepts
of adaptive rationality developed by the Venezuelans. Friedmann
brings this out in a footnote that should not be overlooked (Chapter II, note 31, pp. 78–79). Reading between the lines, one might
suspect that in Venezuela Friedmann had the opportunity to un-
learn some things he had previously learned under Tugwell at the
University of Chicago.

Forty years ago, in an essay more philosophic than economic,
John Maynard Keynes pointed out an interesting paradox concerning the development of national economic planning in democratic
countries. "Material poverty provides the incentive to change precisely where there is very little margin for experiments. Material
prosperity removes the incentive just when it might be safe to take
a chance. Europe lacks the means, America the will to make a
move." [14]

In Venezuela, the paradox has been avoided by the fortuitous
combination of material poverty of the masses, vast oil resources
that provide a margin for experiment, and resourceful leaders with
the will to develop new means of action. This, too, has international
implications. Just as French methods of democratic planning are
being adapted outside France, Venezuelan methods may be helpful outside Venezuela.

More specifically, Venezuelan planners—while still facing major
problems in their own country—have an important role to play in
advising and assisting in economic development. Their pragmatic,
action-oriented style and their experience in relating planning to
annual program budgets could be of tremendous help not only in
Latin America but also in Asia and Africa. Nor are these qualities
of concern only to the so-called developing nations. I have already had the pleasure of seeing Tejera Paris in action at an international planning conference in Warsaw. Men like Hurtado have
skills and experience that are also relevant to the dialogue of consensus building in a highly pluralistic society such as the United
States of America. I should like to see such men called upon to
advise the U.S. government on many of its planning problems. Per-

[14] John Maynard Keynes, *The End of Laissez-Faire* (London: Hogarth
Press, 1926), pp. 53–54.

haps some day we may yet "abandon the myopic, one-way-street concept of technical assistance which sends American 'experts' on economic development to many other countries and seems to rule out the idea that we too may have something to learn from foreign experts. . . ." [15]

BERTRAM M. GROSS

Syracuse, New York
Autumn 1965

[15] Bertram M. Gross, "New Look for the Employment Act," *Challenge* (February 1963), p. 13.

Background

A YEAR OF DECISION

The summer and fall of 1963 were seasons of intense political debate in Venezuela. A half-decade of conscientious democratic rule was drawing to a close. National elections were scheduled for December, and seven candidates contended for the highest office.[1] In gatherings up and down the country, from cosmopolitan centers to the remotest jungle outpost, all the important issues of national life were being scrutinized and argued.

The debate itself, though acrimonious, was peaceful; still, it was conducted in an atmosphere of extreme intranquility. A planned campaign of terror, directed by the Communist Party of Venezuela (PCV) and the illegal Revolutionary Movement of the Left (MIR) but principally carried out by the Armed Forces of National Liberation (FALN), mounted in intensity and daring as election day approached. Its immediate purpose was to spread fear and disorder and, if possible, to disrupt the constitutional processes of government. Bridges were blown up, warehouses set aflame, oil pipelines dynamited, and on one occasion members of the American Military Mission were ignominiously disrobed and publicly exposed to ridicule. But in spite of this staccato succession of violence, life continued in its normal routines. The extreme left wing appeared to have been effectively isolated in public opinion and was acting wholly beyond the pale of legality. Repressive measures could be selectively enforced upon a diminutive segment of the population without substantially infringing on the general freedoms of speech, assembly, and movement. The rest of the country was indeed not

1

so much torn by ideological dissension as united in the major national goals of the present generation: the strengthening of a democratic social order and the achievement of a sustained high rate of economic growth.

One example must stand for many. When in the fall of 1963 the government arrested Communist leaders who had previously enjoyed congressional immunity, opposition parties did not withdraw from the elections as some had thought they would. And the great debate continued. It turned chiefly on the issue of which among the several competing parties would be the most successful in promoting national development, relieving gross poverty and unemployment, expanding industry, and hastening agrarian reform. In this debate the national economic plan served as a major catalyst.

A completely revised version of the *Plan de La Nación, 1963– 1966* was published earlier in the year. Of very high technical quality, it was widely regarded as the most competent national planning report in the Americas. Although it had been drafted undoubtedly with an eye on the coming elections, it was no narrow partisan program. Transcending party doctrine, it concentrated on the main parameters of national life: growth, stability, and social welfare. This emphatic national orientation was something relatively new in Venezuelan experience, suggesting a willingness to compromise conflict rather than engage in a sterile contest of irreconcilable doctrines. President Rómulo Betancourt went so far as to express a hope that the plan might be a guide to the succeeding government and so provide for basic continuity in public policy.[2]

The plan became immediately the object of intensive public review. In the months following its publication—significantly, it had appeared as a loosely bound document in a cheap photo-offset reproduction—scarcely a day passed without some comment in the press that bore directly on the questions the plan had raised. The over-all growth rate, unemployment, the regional problem—these and many more topics were examined within the terms of reference established by the plan. Sharp criticism of the plan analysis and program proposals was voiced. But the critics were constrained to make their assertions reasonably factual and to consider the basic interrelationships of economic life as portrayed in the structure of the plan itself.

Substantive aspects of the plan were the overriding concern at the annual meeting of the powerful Federation of Chambers of Commerce and Industry (Fedecámeras), which was held in the city of Barcelona during June. Significantly, the meeting rejected the proposal of a conservative minority to accept what amounted to a "counterplan" of its own, a statement that would have opposed the government program principally on points of doctrine. Instead, it supported a proposal to participate in a joint standing committee, which, with representatives from government and other private sectors, would provide for continuing assessment of the national plan. For the first time in the history of the nation, a formal procedure for consultations between business and government was to be established. The plan would be the instrument of conjunction. But more important than the plan itself was to be an ongoing dialogue between the private and public sectors, a dialogue that would be disciplined by econometric models to insure not only the internal consistency of alternative proposals but also adherence to the major goals of public policy.

The decision by Fedecámeras represented a major change in the attitudes of the organization and was the result of a long factional struggle for internal control. It is too early to predict how well the decision will be implemented and whether it signifies, as suggested here, a new era in relations between business and government. But there can be little doubt that the decision itself represents a major achievement of planning in Venezuela to date. From the very inception of national planning, the intent, if not always the practice, was to draw business and other elements of the private sector into the heart and fibers of the planning process. How this was finally accomplished is a major theme of the present study.

A second principal concern is the uses of planning. What is the relation of "manifest" to "latent" functions in planning? Broadly speaking, the former have to do with the achievement of greater functional rationality in economic decisions and an accelerated rate of economic growth, the latter with the social consequences of adopting formal planning mechanisms. It will be shown that the latent functions of planning may, under some conditions, be even more important to society than any gains in functional rationality. Goal achievement is not the only criterion by which success in planning may be measured.

The study is concerned with the experience of only one country at a critical juncture in its history. Much of the detail reported will certainly be unique. Yet the hope seems justified that we may learn from this experience, that it will tell us something significant about planning as a form of social action. If a satisfactory process theory of planning should ever be written, it will have to be grounded in empirically verified social behavior. This basic conviction motivated the present study and informed all stages of the analysis.

SOCIETY IN TRANSITION

Extending from the Caribbean coast into the equatorial regions of the Amazon, Venezuela is a moderately sized country of about eight million.[3] Until the discovery of large quantities of oil in the early twenties, its economy resembled that of many other South American countries. It exhibited a traditional agrarian pattern with specialization in export crops, such as coffee and cacao, as well as in cattle. The shift to oil and the subsequent expansion of manufacturing eradicated this order and, in less than a generation, propelled the country toward becoming a modern, urban-based civilization. By 1961 nearly 60 per cent of the population was living in cities of over five thousand and the metropolitan area of Caracas alone counted well over one million inhabitants.

Oil was the shaping force of transformation. Even today its contribution to the economy continues to be major, accounting, as it does, for more than one-fifth of the national product, continuing as the chief source of foreign exchange earnings, and being principally responsible for the high per capita income of the country. On the basis of income alone, and relative to its population, Venezuela is today the wealthiest nation in South America and compares favorably with a number of Western European economies. Structurally, however, its economy exhibits many anomalies, juxtaposing conditions of extreme backwardness with elements of great sophistication.

The critical turning point was 1921, when the great oil well, "Los Barros No. 2," came into production on the eastern shores of Lake Maracaibo. In the succeeding four decades Venezuela moved rapidly from exclusive dependence on oil to an autonomous national life based on a reasonably diversified economic structure. Social dualism characterized by a tightly knit power elite at the top and a more or less homogeneous mass of peasants below it gave way to a complex structure of highly differentiated interest groups. In the political realm this shift was accompanied by the substitution of a broadly based multiparty structure for a strong-man regime run almost exclusively for the benefit of the elite. In more specific language, this period of roughly a single generation witnessed the rise of an urban middle class with new values and a commitment to obliterating the traditional agrarian-military order.

The appellation "middle class" has been much misused and remains at best a rather vague description of an extremely complex social phenomenon. But in Venezuela "middle class" has a rather special connotation, referring there to a residual category of occupational types wedged in between the "oligarchy" of large landowners, military castes, bankers, and large importers on the one hand and the *lumpenproletariat* of landless peasants and unskilled urban workers on the other. This leaves, to be precise, the mass of white collar and skilled service workers, small tradesmen and farmers, as well as elitist groups of professionals, intellectuals, industrialists, and university students. These new elites were relatively deprived groups in the sense that significant positions of political authority and power were denied them. Although lacking a pronounced class consciousness, their swelling numbers—a consequence of rapidly paced urbanization—gave them a sense of internal unity and, above all, a sense of mission. Their members regarded themselves as the phalanx of modernity. Politically, they claimed to be speaking for *all* Venezuelans, except the oligarchs. This stance assured them of popular support.

During the early period of oil exploration, however, General Juan Vicente Gómez still presided over the country as a master would over his *hacienda,* disposing of his subjects' lives and fortunes with nearly absolute authority. From the western and eastern provinces, oil revenues poured into the national treasury at the "center" and hence passed into the pockets of the interlocking directorate that effectively controlled the national economy. Much of the money was spent on high living and extravagant construction jobs, for the most part in Caracas itself. Small concern was given to the building up of other economic sectors, since needs could readily be satisfied through importation. Agricultural production declined, and most of the population was kept in misery and ignorance, lest they turn restless and demanding. Not unreasonably, rural population migrated in large numbers to the cities. Caracas alone quintupled in size over a twenty-five-year period.

But the seemingly invincible position of the oligarchy was being subtly undermined by the irreversible process of urbanization that its economic and social policies had unleashed. Stirrings of discontent came to public notice as early as 1928, when a group of student leaders, outspokenly critical of the regime, were arrested. Among them was Rómulo Betancourt and a number of others who, to this day, continue to play prominent roles in the political life of the nation. On that distant "Día de Estudiantes" Venezuela's social revolution began.

General Gómez died in 1935 and was replaced by another officer of the oligarchy's own choosing. The new middle class leadership was still too weak to attempt an independent bid for power. The following nine years saw a gradual liberalization of political institutions and some efforts at structural reform. But the pace was altogether too slow to satisfy the opposition, who maintained relentless pressure against the established order whose tradition-bound, self-serving attitudes it held in deep contempt. The Democratic Action party (AD) was founded during the Second World War by Rómulo Betancourt and others. It prided itself on being a multiclass party, but its platform, judged by standards then prevailing, was clearly revolutionary in intent. Its goals included universal suffrage, secret ballot, free elections, professionalism in the army, national autonomy, agrarian reform, industrial diversification, regional development, and social justice.

War had counseled a strategy of restraint. But no sooner was the surrender of the Axis announced, than a coalition of Democratic Action and vaguely disgruntled junior officers deposed the government of General Medina Angarita and, under the skillful leadership of Rómulo Betancourt, installed a revolutionary junta composed largely of civilians (October 1945). This move must be interpreted as the first serious attempt by spokesmen of the rising urban middle class to pass from theory to action, to wrest effective power from the hidebound oligarchy, and set in motion a process of socioeconomic transformation that was conceived in its own image.

But the victory was celebrated prematurely. The new leadership had yet to master the art of politics which involved something more than the drafting of "progressive" legislation. The oligarchy had been powerless to prevent the ascent of its rival, but its resources had by no means been exhausted. Expectantly, it waited on the sidelines for an opportunity to strike back.

The new government acted rashly and with considerable naivete. It assumed, for instance, the existence of powerful popular support for its own policies, when strong emotional commitment to a democratic order was in fact wanting. In one sense the timing of the revolution had been opportune, coinciding, as it did, with the flurry of postwar enthusiasm for peace, plenty, and social justice. But a genuine crisis situation did not exist in Venezuela, and reasons for urgent structural reforms were not widely perceived. Falsely regarding itself as leading a massive popular movement, the junta deemed itself sufficiently secure to lash out simultaneously against both military and civilian elements of the oligarchy. It alienated the officer corps by ignoring its demands for preferential treatment and by failing to consult it on critical decisions; at the same time, it threatened the landlords with immediate expropriation. For a while some progress along these lines was made. A new constitution was ratified in 1947 and a president duly elected the following year. But his government lasted only a few months. In the autumn of 1948 a coup d'état, sanctioned if not organized by the oligarchy, was successful. With a dramatic show of strength Colonel Marcos Pérez Jiménez initiated a decade of the most ruthless dictatorship the country had ever known. It is worth noting that, contrary to more optimistic expectations, the public accepted this restoration of the old order rather calmly. Three years had not been sufficient to demonstrate the superiority of democratic institutions.

Colonel Pérez Jiménez was a man of small imagination and neither skillful nor subtle as a politician. He was also a ruthless autocrat, backed by a brutally efficient chief of police. Jails and penal colonies were soon crowded with political prisoners, torture chambers were kept busy around the clock, and those among the opposition who survived went either underground or into exile.

Economically the country fared surprisingly well during the decade, considering the gross corruption and total irresponsibility of the regime. Under the impact of the Suez crisis and the Korean war, oil exports flourished, and manufacturing output spurted ahead at better than 10 per cent a year. But as the years wore on economic prosperity in a handful of cities was insufficient to balance the ex-

cesses, mismanagement, and plain venality of the regime. The political situation was becoming intolerable. Early in January 1958
the breaking-point of sufferance was reached. In a spontaneous out-
burst of anger and frustration the people of Caracas took to the
streets; soldiers made common cause with civilians and in a matter
of hours brought on the collapse of a government that had been
totally discredited. For those participating in the events it was a
moment of supreme catharsis. Strangers embraced each other,
laughed, and danced in the streets. When Pérez Jiménez fled the
country in a private plane, the prison gates were thrown open and
a provisional junta took charge once more. This time, however, the
victory of the new middle class seemed more secure. Later in the
year the Democratic Action party, under Rómulo Betancourt, won
the national election over three contending parties and inaugurated
a half-decade of frequently hectic but democratic reform.

   To claim early success for this undertaking would be unwar-
ranted. The oligarchy certainly did not suddenly vanish from the
scene. But at least for the time being, it was effectively demobilized
and its return to power is now regarded as exceedingly improbable.
The reasons for this conclusion are complex and had best be stated
separately.

   A decade of heavy-handed dictatorship has widely discredited
the ability of the oligarchy to lead the country toward the fulfillment
of national aspirations. Not only is the oligarchy wholly lacking in
popular sympathy, but its implied ideological position, adequate
perhaps for a simpler social structure, has become intellectually dis-
reputable.

   The military, always essential to a prospective comeback of the
oligarchy, has been treated with great consideration by the government. Its fortunes have fared well in the budget, and the comfort
of its officers has been well looked after. Professionalism has been
stressed and the rising wave of terrorism after 1961 provided a
convenient outlet for a demonstration of military skill. Ideologically,
moreover, the military appears to be increasingly divided. Not only
has a polarization of political attitudes occurred, but the years since
1958 have seen the rise of reform elements among the officer corps
who are supporting efforts to improve economic and social conditions in the country. Spreading liberal sentiments of this kind were
apparently instrumental in maintaining a balance of military power
during the period of President Betancourt's government.

Further internal division within the military was accomplished by transforming the old National Guard into a fourth military branch, the Armed Forces of Cooperation (FAC), which was successfully employed against mutinous units of the Army at Puerto Cabello, and of the Navy at Carúpano. For all these reasons, then, concerted military action against the government, while not totally inconceivable, appears today far more difficult to accomplish than at any time previously.

On looking about in the modern, postrevolutionary era, the once all-powerful oligarchy suddenly discovered that it had been reduced to the more modest dimensions of a simple pressure group, one among many that were seeking satisfaction through political action. The old dualistic social structure had disappeared beyond recall. Since the early forties, ten political parties had sprung into existence. Workers, farmers, and peasants were variously organized into unions and associations. Professional associations (of engineers, economists, lawyers, etc.) abounded. Chambers of Commerce and Industry were loosely knit into a federation. Other organizations, such as Pro-Venezuela, cut across occupational lines in their advocacy of national programs. In brief, where only a lethargic, diffuse mass that could be easily manipulated from the top had existed but a few decades earlier, there was now an abundance of publics, reasonably well organized for exerting political influence. The oligarchy would have to learn the rules of the new game; its erstwhile ability for autonomous and irresponsible action had been lost beyond redemption. Its defeat at the Barcelona meeting of Fedecámeras, alluded to earlier, may be read as a measure of its general impotency.

Individual members of the oligarchy, to the extent that they had not sought refuge in pouting exile overseas or were engaged in fantasy constructions, moved in skillfully to exploit new opportunities for enterprise, chiefly outside the agricultural sector. Some of them became powerful entrepreneurs in their own right and identified with a new constellation of interests that led them to support many of the basic policies of the government. Except for a few diehards, the erstwhile oligarchy is no longer genuinely interested in a counterrevolution of the right. Its existential position has shifted.

The rise of Communism posed a common threat and caused the interests of both the middle class and the oligarchy to converge at least in part. This was facilitated by a split within the Democratic

Action party on the issue of Cuban recognition. As the left wing of the party regrouped itself into new political constellations in opposition to the government, the hard core of Democratic Action grew inevitably more conservative and consequently more acceptable to the oligarchy. While the former oligarchy might not wish to perpetuate the party in office, it would certainly not move against the government in a moment of acute political crisis.

The years since 1958 have been difficult. The revolution coincided with a sharp decline in world markets for petroleum. Reduced oil exports were immediately translated into smaller government revenues. Public expenditures were curtailed with disastrous results, particularly in the construction industry. More than a hundred thousand workers suddenly found themselves without jobs. The double collapse of the oil and construction booms that had marked the preceding decade pushed all other economic indicators downward. The spreading sense of depression was reinforced by large-scale capital flight and the departure of thousands of foreign immigrants who had previously occupied key economic positions. Unemployment reached dangerously high levels estimated at 14 per cent of the labor force as late as 1962. Although the economy appeared to have made some recovery by that time, earlier levels were not quickly recovered.

The problems confronting the Betancourt government during its term of office were evidently manifold and interlocking, but at least two may be identified as posing an ultimate challenge to the ingenuity of national leaders.

The first may be described as a lack of political consensus. A North American with his pragmatic outlook would probably dismiss a problem so formulated out-of-hand. Consensus for him need reach no further than agreement on procedures. For the rest, there is the usual give-and-take whenever concrete issues are involved. But Venezuelans do not see their problem in this light. The country had not been prepared for the sudden appearance of a large number of political and other interest groups, each advancing its own cause in disregard of the concerns of others. Nor was it accustomed to unmitigated freedom of expression and action. The democratic order was neither firmly entrenched nor fully legitimated. To many Venezuelans, therefore, absence of consensus signified a lack of national unity, a lack of those organic bonds of comradeship which had sustained them during long years of illegal political activity, but had now withered and been lost. Surely, such expectations were misplaced. Surely, every unity effort to date has suffered shipwreck, sometimes even prior to being launched. But this failure to read the problem correctly posed the danger of suicidal conflict, as doctrine opposed doctrine, and prolonged economic depression slowly brought back the wish for a strong-willed government, albeit a "progressive" one, that would, with simple and clear pronouncements, cut through the entanglement of uncertainty, tedious discussion, untidiness, and shifting alignments inherent in democratic procedures. Terrorist acts and annual attempts at rebellion were a disturbing, demoralizing element in the situation, and served to heighten existing social tensions.[4]

The second major problem was economic development. It had at least three aspects: the reduction and eventual elimination of unemployment, diversification of the country's economic base, and achievement of some form of interregional balance in the levels of living.

Unemployment was primarily a political issue. Unless the growth rate could be stepped up to somewhere within the range of 10 per cent, it was unlikely that unemployment could be made to disappear rapidly. For unemployment was not so much the result of "excessive" rural-urban migration as a control upon the rate of migration itself. Although the problem was to find that equilibrium rate of unemployment at which a normal rate of absorption into the work force would occur, the issue was not understood this way. Public ethics supported a policy of *full* employment, rather than an equilibrium rate of unemployment. Any government would be highly vulnerable if it failed to make full employment of the country's available labor force a high priority objective. Combating unemployment had been an important element in national policy since the days of President Larrazábal's "Emergency Plan" of 1958; by 1962, with an official unemployment rate of 14 per cent, it had become the overriding issue.

Diversification was regarded as a survival value in an economy whose mainstay continued to be an exhaustible resource. Long-term projections in the national plan foresaw the ultimate decline both in the absolute and relative contribution that oil would make to the economy. This made the shift of base to other resources a necessity.

Industrialization was primarily affected. In 1959 manufacturing had contributed only 15 per cent of the gross national product and was concentrated mainly in food products, textiles, and construction materials. The new doctrine was to establish a heavy industrial sector that would reduce Venezuela's dependence on imported iron and steel, heavy machinery, consumer durables, and chemical products.

The problem of regional balance was closely related. The large concentrations of population, wealth, and political power in the Caracas region have already been noted. This was widely regarded as an evil. For one thing, the Democratic Action government derived most of its support from the provinces and consequently had a political debt to discharge. Beyond this partisan view, however, there were other considerations. For instance, the goal of building a modern, integrated nation-state was inconsistent with exclusive attention to the development of Caracas and the central region. The latter had been the policy of the oligarchy and was an untenable alternative. Moreover, the periphery had potential resources that could be brought into play to strengthen the economy's over-all performance. The most striking instance of this could be found in southeastern Venezuela, where vast iron ore deposits and a large potential power supply offered the means for establishing a major industrial complex in the interior provinces. The government undertook an ambitious development program in the Guayana region, an example whose significance was not lost on other areas. Demands were soon voiced from different parts of the country for an equally generous treatment. Great discrepancies in the levels of living and growth rates were thought to be not only unjust but dangerous to political stability. The world showed altogether too many examples of peripheral revolts for this argument to be breezily dismissed.[5] Solutions would not be easy. But the regional issue had clearly become a matter of great urgency and was being widely debated during the 1963 election campaign.

National economic planning was institutionalized late in 1958. Over the years it has become ever more widely accepted as a major policy-shaping device. Critics have been of three kinds. The neo-liberals wanted to abolish planning altogether; the Marxists advocated eliminating the private sector in favor of planning on the Russian or Chinese models; and various centrist groups, while accepting the general framework of planning, sought to modify the order of priorities and the means adopted.[6] The neoliberals were totally ineffectual in their holy war against planning; the Marxist comment was irrelevant and, in any event, presupposed a socialist revolution; there remained only the debate on the merits of the current planning effort, and this indeed became a key issue during the election campaign.[7] It stands to the credit of the planning system that the debate was carried on within the logical and factual framework of the plan itself. Even the most rhetorical of appeals had to demonstrate a modicum of rationality if it wanted to be heard. Every major party had its professional economic advisors. A good part of the campaign was consequently reduced to a debate of alternative patterns of resource allocation. This proved no doubt a somewhat sobering experience.

The Origins of Planning

BASIC PLANNING LEGISLATION

Early in 1958, a few months after the provisional government had taken office, a "Preparatory Commission for a National System of Coordination and Governmental Planning" was appointed to draft a proposal and the necessary legislation. The commission was headed by Enrique Tejera Paris, an outstanding social scientist and trusted collaborator of Rómulo Betancourt.[1]

The full title of the commission was significant; it reflected the basic philosophy that would guide its members throughout their work. It stressed the idea that planning, rather than being the exclusive responsibility of a single agency, involves a multitude of decision points which must be linked into a system. And it made "coordination" coequal with planning. What distinguished national planning from other forms of decision-making was, accordingly, a method by which a diversity of interests and programs might be welded into a total conception. Individual effort was to be guided by an overarching set of national goals.

Equally significant was the membership of the commission. All major political parties were represented on it. The system of planning was meant to transcend partisan interests; its inspiration was to be drawn from the self-evident, critical needs of the nation. Just as political differences had been suppressed in the common struggle against the dictatorship, so the nation would stand together (it was hoped) in the greater contest with misery and injustice that lay ahead. Such terms as "harmonious action" and "unity" abounded in the final document that was produced.

14

The report was submitted in the fall of 1958, and legislation establishing the Central Office of Coordination and Planning (COR-DIPLAN) was enacted on December 30th.[2]

It may be worth noting that national planning had some important precedents in Venezuela. Several of the ministries had formal planning operations, as with respect to transportation, public health, and urban form. Responsibility for general economic policy was divided among institutions which included the Central Bank, the National Economic Council of the Ministry of Development, the Policy Staff of the Foreign Ministry, and the Budget Council. What was plainly missing, however, was an effective method for policy and program coordination. The commission report asserted:

> At issue is not the creation of a new minstry nor a costly bureaucratic apparatus duplicating what already exists. It is rather to forge a common habit of prevision and to sustain long-term policies in a coordinated fashion. In short, it is to introduce a new dimension in government, opposed to improvisation, to the neglect of investments, and to the wastage of resources.[3]

The new planning act, however, represented something more than the incremental improvement suggested in the preceding passage. It signified a major structural change in the method of public administration. A review of some of the principal provisions of the act may lead to a better understanding of the conception of planning that was intended.

The task of planning

> Basic to planning and coordination . . . is a labor of analysis, projection, and general goal formulation, complemented by consultation with the public and private sectors, as well as the preparation of a program-budget. Planning and coordination imply the harmonization of the pace of development and the form of project implementation, in addition to monitoring of the results, as determined by the national executive.[4]

Planning was here construed as a technical-scientific activity, forward-looking in its orientation, and responsible for the formulation of national goals. It would involve a process of mutual consultation, both within the government and between the public and private sectors. Its real pay-off, however, was to be the program-budget which would relate the physical to the fiscal plan, and lead directly into the phase of project and program implementation. Congressional review of planning would thus continue to focus on the budget legislated into law each year. In this there was no fundamental change from earlier practice, except that the budget itself would be presented in a greatly improved form. In short, the span of planning was to extend from long-range goal formulation to individual projects, but the weight of emphasis was clearly on a more immediate planning horizon. With respect to projects, planning was assigned a general responsibility for setting the order of priorities, arranging projects over a time sequence, determining the manner of their implementation, and observing their consequences in a continuous feedback process of information.

Defining the planners

Planning legislation was intended to apply to all officials, at all levels of government, who "have a specific responsibility for the preparation of work programs, related investigations, and monitoring the implementation of these programs for information and by order of an immediate superior." [5] But, "The supreme coordination of planning and the implementation of government programs rests with the president of the republic and the Council of Ministers." [6] And, "The Central Office of Coordination and Planning is herewith created and is intended to assist the president of the republic and the Council of Ministers." [7]

According to these provisions, planning and coordination were thought to be government-wide functions. In a certain sense—though it is not clear how far this meaning was intended—government officials throughout the hierarchy of command were charged with responsibility for planning. As a minimum, it was suggested that each major government agency should have a "little CORDI-PLAN" for coordinating its own operations. The planning act further implied that planning, coordination, and implementation were merely different phases of the same activity; they were conceptually indivisible.

Responsibility for over-all coordination and policy-making was to remain with the president and his cabinet. The Central Planning Office was to be exclusively employed in a staff capacity, as the principal advisor in economic matters to the chief executive. It was to have no program or operating responsibilities of its own.

Planning as a system

> The national executive, acting through the Central Office of Coordination and Planning, will stimulate the creation of coordination and programming organisms in the several states and municipalities, as well as of interstate or intermunicipal organisms, within a general plan of administrative coordination.[8]

In addition, CORDIPLAN was given responsibility for coordinating regional planning. Its function here was "to propose the general framework for physical and spatial planning on a national scale and to coordinate regional and urban planning in accordance with the stated guidelines through the appropriate planning organizations." [9]

The system concept of planning was thus applied not only to national ministries but also to territorially organized units of government. Economic planning was to be linked to spatial planning, just as project planning was to be carefully related to the budget process. State and city planning were not, however, made obligatory. CORDIPLAN was charged merely with giving encouragement to spatial planning endeavors and with formulating the over-all framework for coordination in the event that spatially decentralized planning ever became a reality.

The citations above are only fragments of the basic planning law, but they succeed in conveying its essential spirit. The question arises why national planning came to be institutionalized in this way. Why should there be national planning at all? Why did it take this form? And why was it created at this particular juncture in the history of the country?

Three answers will be proposed, each of which will give only a partial explanation. To begin, planning was introduced as one element in a new middle class ideology which found expression in the concept of a "development society." Besides planning, the ideology included nationalism and economic development among its principal terms. Since the revolution of 1958 reflected chiefly urban middle class values and the ascendancy of this class over a backward-looking oligarchy, planning came to be introduced in a symbolic way as part of an over-all ideological orientation. Second, the probability of its acceptance as a method for arriving at public decisions was enhanced by a number of historical and personal reasons, which are detailed below. These are historically unique and help explain the form Venezuela's experiment in national planning assumed. Third, the adoption of national planning by the provisional government late in 1958 was practically assured by a widespread crisis of frustration which sprang from a deep desire to solve the country's problems in a hurry in the face of immense obstacles of every possible variety. Each of these answers will be taken up in turn.

A DEVELOPMENT SOCIETY

By the time they arrived in a position of national power, the leaders of Venezuela's social revolution had come to embrace a mystique that was singularly appropriate to their time and place. Lack of an adequate ideology had contributed to the success of the counterrevolution a decade earlier, when only a few voices were raised in defense of the frail democratic order that had tenuously established a first beachhead in Venezuela. Ideas of liberalism and piecemeal reform were no longer able to draw strong emotional commitment. In a major policy statement during the election campaign of 1963, one of the leading presidential candidates sharply reflected this disillusionment with phrases that had become worn out by overuse. "We've had enough," proclaimed Arturo Uslar Pietri, "of all that fine talk about public liberties, civil liberties, constitutionality, human rights, and revolution—a revolution that no one bothers to define nor really knows what it is." [10] The statement is significant because it came from one of Venezuela's leading intellectuals, a man of thoroughly democratic persuasion. Uslar Pietri made his appeal—and it would seem quite successfully—to "independents" who had grown tired of established political parties and their never-ending machinations. The president might preach democracy, Uslar Pietri suggested, but the real issue was economic development and a "fair deal" for the poor and ignorant and un-skilled.

His sentiments no more than echoed a widespread popular at-titude which, to a degree, had already been present in the period from 1945 to 1948 when the Democratic party first attempted to engineer a social revolution from the top. Eighteen years later, there was no question that an ideology was needed that would rally poli-tical support for revolutionary sentiments and justify the claims of middle class elitist groups to guide the destiny of the nation. The ideology of a development society was to be their ultimate source of legitimacy to govern.[11]

To these considerations must be added the fact that the defi-nition of one's ideological position is still widely regarded in Vene-zuela, and indeed throughout South America, as a sign of one's authenticity as a person. And just as individuals are expected to bring ideas and actions into a perfect coincidence, political parties and professional or business organizations feel obliged to rationalize their behavior in terms of broad philosophical propositions. Vene-zuelans do not act more in the conformity with predefined doctrine than do other people. The successful Venezuelan politician can be as pragmatic as his North American counterpart who, with equal conviction, will disclaim adherence to any ideological tendency. Truth is probably found in an intermediate position where ideas and opportunity are joined in action. Nevertheless, the folkways of Venezuelan political life cannot be ignored. To lack an ideological position is to be discredited in advance. The new middle class, therefore, needed an ideology that could be successfully employed in political disputes with Marxist doctrine, which was widely known and well articulated. Not to have done so in 1958 would have created a vacuum of ideas that the Marxists would have quickly filled. The oligarchy, of course, claimed no particular ideology as its own and had been obliged to maintain itself by a combination of force and personal charisma.

What we shall call the ideology of the new middle class was de-fined by a few intellectuals in a remarkable document, the "Doctrine and Program of Democratic Action," which was adopted by the party in August 1958.[12] Though by no means a unified statement, the basic message comes through unimpaired. The ideology was rooted in the concept of a "development society," a society wholly committed to "progress" in all phases of its life. In this commitment it reflected a set of pervasive modernist values: an affirmation of change and unlimited progress; an implicit trust in the powers of science and technology to mold and master man's environment; an assertion of the primacy of substance over form, performance over ascription; a sense of egalitarian justice; an assertion of the moral obligation of some formal participation in the political process.[13] To develop a country in the modern sense implies a steady movement toward the realization of these values. Neither the values themselves nor the concept of a development society is uniquely middle class in origin, but every modern political movement has had to adopt them to its own purposes and needs. In this the leadership of Venezuela's social revolution proved to be no exception.

Nationalism, economic development, and planning were the key concepts in terms of which the ideology was expressed.

By nationalism was meant the overriding value of the national interest as the highest public good. Group- and class-centered policies were emphatically rejected and replaced by national objectives. But, given the emerging social structure of Venezuela, it was evident that the national interest could be defined only by accepting pluralism as a condition of political action. Nationalism therefore implied an inclusive political process in which competing interests would have to be arbitrated. This emphasis on the nation, its progress and its welfare, further suggested that the several regions of the country would have to be more fully integrated into the national economy. If a balance had to be struck among different social interests, diverse regional interests had to be brought into a similar equilibrium. By a national economy was meant an interregional economy.

A second meaning of nationalism was "autonomy," the elimination of foreign influence, particularly of the oil corporations, over government policy. The shaping of policy was to be done *by* Venezuelans *for* Venezuelans, with the "national interest"—however defined—as an ultimate criterion of choice.

Nationalism must be clearly distinguished from traditional patriotism. Like many other countries, Venezuela has sought to find a source of present strength in a mystique of the past, in this case symbolized by the heroic figure of Simón Bolívar, the father of the country. In the new ideology, however, nationalism was no longer backward-looking and traditionalist but oriented toward the future. It may have lacked profound symbols, unless national goals could be said to have served in that role, and it was vaguely defined. But its very appeal derived in part from the looseness of its meaning, which allowed varying interpretations without impairing the value of the ideology itself.

The second element of the new middle class ideology was economic development. This was a multifaceted idea signifying over-all economic expansion, improved welfare, and modernization of economic life. Its concrete manifestations were advocacy of diversified resource and industrial development; further rapid urbanization; emphasis on the achievement of high educational and health standards; eradication of poverty in all its forms; and creation of opportunities for unrestrained upward mobility.

The core of the idea of economic development was expressed most succinctly in a statement on national goals drafted by the presidency on the occasion of the eighteenth annual meeting of Fedecámeras in 1962.[14] It effectively summarized earlier thinking and has since been widely quoted in government publications. The relevant paragraphs may be cited in full:

> Planning which has recently been initiated endeavors to establish a comprehensive framework for the economy in which the efforts of all sectors are harmoniously integrated so as to achieve, in the interest of the nation as a whole, the fundamental goals which have been established, including:
>
> 1. The highest level of welfare for all Venezuelans, to be achieved through full employment of the labor force and an equitable distribution of the nation's wealth, using the expanding resources of the several regions of the country in the most efficient manner possible; and
>
> 2. Economic independence, through an adequate diversification of the economy and the optimal growth of the national product, and to be achieved especially through an improved application of public revenues derived from the country's just participation in the extractive industry.[15]

The third, and final, element of the new doctrine was planning, which was advanced as the instrumentality for the rapid attainment of national objectives. "Planning," proclaimed Rómulo Betancourt on the occasion of his fifth presidential message, "is the inevitable slogan of our time." [16] Frequent references to planning had appeared in the Democratic Action Program of 1958.[17] It might be argued that unreasonable hopes were placed in the efficacy of planning. Its use frequently suggested almost magical powers that would instantly resolve the most intractable of problems. Such was the implicit faith in planning, whose internal structure as a process was correctly understood by only a small number of insiders.

The significance of planning as an ideology may be expressed as the first terms in a series of dichotomies: [18]

a. *rationality (efficient means-ends relationships)* vs. political irrationality;

b. *hierarchical order* vs. random disorder;

c. *wholeness (comprehensiveness, coordination)* vs. fragmentation in decision-making;

d. *moral neutrality* vs. subjectivism;

e. *responsible government participation in economic life* vs. unrestrained free enterprise.

In short, the ideological component of planning was its public image as an efficient instrumentality which, in the skilled hands of economists and technocrats, would quickly lead to the fulfillment of national aspirations. That this image had little to do with the reality of planning, even as instituted in Venezuela itself, bore little relevance to its force as an idea.

The three elements of middle class ideology were closely interlinked, and may be visualized as the three points of a triangle at whose apex stood nationalism as the highest good and whose base rested on principles of economic development and planning. None of the elements could be removed without impairing the significance of the total conception. Economic development was needed to achieve the purposes of nationalism and in particular the goal of national autonomy. Planning was an instrumental value to both purposes.

What made the ideology so attractive to the new middle class leadership as a means for obtaining political support was that it pointed to a convergence of class and national interests in several strategic areas of concern. If the middle class was served by industrialization and the creation of mass markets, for example, so was the nation as a whole. Both objectives required for their attainment the notion of national autonomy and economic independence (protective tariffs), large-scale income redistribution (mass markets), decentralization and diversification (industrial development), and an open society. All these were clearly in the national interest as well. Political debates in 1963 revealed little basic disagreement with these general purposes.

The idea of an open society as a specific middle class value deserves separate comment. It is the explanation of much seemingly paradoxical behavior, including the supreme paradox—at least in Marxist terms—of the advocacy of policies by a "class" which might frequently go counter to its immediate material interests. The Marxists might see this as one of the "internal contradictions" of the bourgeoisie. But in point of fact, it helps explain the tolerant attitude of the middle class, its willingness to compromise issues in a pragmatic way, and its leanings toward a pluralistic social order. The middle class advocated an open society—in Venezuela as elsewhere—because it believed in a vision of an essentially *classless* society, based on mass consumption and private property. The millenium would accordingly arrive when everyone had become "middle class" in his income, tastes, and philosophy. Nothing would serve the immediate interests of the middle class better than having everyone employed, enjoying a comfortable income, living in "decent" communities, owning some property—a house, consumer hardware, a car, some stocks or bonds, and voting in annual elections. These are, of course, precisely the values of Everyman. Its irresistible appeal has consequently turned the idea of a development society into one of the great ideological movements of our time. Certainly on Venezuelan ground it was holding its own against stiff Marxist competition.[19]

HISTORICAL CONDITIONS

The inclusion of planning in middle class ideology in no way assured that it would become institutionalized, and it certainly did not prescribe its form. The concept of a "development society" is abroad in most Latin American countries today, but until the "Alliance for Progress" made aid practically contingent on well-constructed national programs, few countries had experimented with national planning in any formal way. If planning was integral to their rhetoric, however, why did not other societies, equally in the throes of middle class revolution, such as Brazil, adopt it? An explanation may be found in historical and personal circumstances that cannot be generalized beyond the boundaries of a particular time and place.

During the thirties, the forerunner of Democratic Action, the National Democratic party (PDN), was an early champion of the idea of planning. But the PDN appears to have had only the vaguest conception of what national planning was about. Its image of planning was loosely derived from what little was then known of Soviet experience. The PDN Program of 1939 called for national economic planning under the title of "Economic Reconstruction of Venezuela." [20] But, at the time, the concept of a development society did not as yet exist, and the vocabulary and method of democratic planning had not been invented.[21] As neither the PDN nor Democratic Action were Marxist parties, however, it is clear that they did not really know what to do with "planning" beyond proclaiming its desirability.

These circumstances help explain why planning was not formally introduced in 1945, when Democratic Action first assumed the responsibilities of government. The fundamental idea of the handful of "angry young men" who rose to power in Venezuela shortly after the war was that of "reconstruction," structural reform, taking substance primarily in new legislation. The idea of sustained planning did not intrude on this conception. It should also be noted that the first basic works in economic development literature did not appear until the early fifties.[22] It was therefore not until the decade of dictatorship that Venezuela's future leaders could recast their ideas in the form of a new ideology and master the art and technics of economic planning.

A key role in this educative process was played by the United Nations Economic Commission for Latin America (ECLA). It was ECLA that fathered the development society as a middle class doctrine. It was ECLA that publicized Latin America's economic plight and asserted a powerful claim with the more advanced economies, principally the United States, for large-scale aid. It was ECLA that promoted a relatively straightforward method of economic programming and demonstrated the political neutrality of the technique. And it was ECLA that trained most of Latin America's leading economists and projected them into positions of eminence.[23] Most recently, in an unusual step for an international organization, the commission even distributed to member governments a document that to all appearances is a manifesto giving the clarion call for social revolution.[24]

ECLA's philosophy had taken shape in a path-breaking study, *The Economic Growth of Latin America and Its Principal Problems*.[25] This led, in 1953, to a report on economic programming which appeared in a revised edition two years later and laid the foundation for subsequent attempts to introduce national planning in Latin America.[26] Programming was ECLA's euphemism for planning and made the idea politically more acceptable by emphasizing its character as an objective technique. The anonymous economists of ECLA's staff write:

> A clear distinction is not always made between the concept of a development program and that of a rigid state control of the economy. Such ambiguity must be dispelled. A programme of economic development is the expression of a simple idea, namely, the desirability of increasing and judiciously regulating capital investment, so that a stronger impetus and greater order may be given to the growth of a country. . . . A programme calls for the firm application of a development policy. But this is possible without shackling private enterprise which may, in fact, be stimulated into undertaking certain activities, and be offered access to essential resources.[27]

The merits of ECLA's approach to programming do not concern us here; they have been debated elsewhere.[28] What is of interest, however, is that ECLA succeeded in making operational a concept of national economic planning within a democratic framework. As it turned out, at least in Venezuela, the method of programming was not quite as important as the consequences that followed its adoption within a specific institutional context. But this should not detract from the fundamental significance of ECLA's work on programming. It is hardly worthwhile to speculate what would have happened had ECLA taken a different course; but the powerful impact its thinking made throughout the continent can scarcely be ignored.

A number of brilliant young Venezuelan economists spent their political exile during the dictatorship as apprentices and teachers with ECLA's staff in Chile. Among them were José Antonio Mayobre, who later occupied the post of finance minister in the provisional government, and Enrique Tejera Paris. Tejera's contribution to the drafting of Venezuela's national planning system has already been mentioned. In May 1957 he presented a report to ECLA on national planning administration based on a review of planning experience in Latin America up to that time.[29] This is very likely the best study of planning organization ever written and was directly responsible for the form of Venezuela's first attempt in this direction. A more extensive analysis of Tejera's main ideas will be presented later. A single quotation may stand here as a summary statement of his basic position.

> More than sporadic action, programming is an attitude. . . . Experience seems to indicate that simply the establishment of a planning unit does not by itself produce the results one might expect, regardless of how many documents and technically irreproachable programs it produces. What is necessary, in addition, is its acceptance by the entire structure and a habit of collaboration in the elaboration of the plans. These conditions require the strong backing of the presidency as well as a mechanism of constant consultation, supported by adequate legislation.[30]

Tejera stressed the social context of planning; he toned down the role of programming as the construction of econometric models.

While Mayobre and Tejera were gathering invaluable experience at ECLA, other prominent Democratic Action leaders and sympathizers went elsewhere for their education. Between 1954 and 1956 Rómulo Betancourt was living in Puerto Rico, where he became a close friend of Governor Muñoz Marín. Under the Governor's influence and from his own observations, Betancourt apparently became convinced of the utility of national economic planning in a democracy. Luís Lander, a close associate of his, was serving as consultant to the Puerto Rican government at the time, having just completed a course in city and regional planning at Harvard University. Lander, who later rose to be president of the Interamerican Society of Planning, lost no opportunities to impress upon the future President of Venezuela the importance of planning, and collected for him basic information on Puerto Rico's experience with "Operation Bootstrap." [31]

Puerto Rican planning and ECLA programming thus came together in a fruitful union. However, the final spark that brought planning to life in Venezuela was the profound social and economic crisis that a decade of willful misrule had generated. True, the economy had flourished during the dictatorship, but this was more the result of favorable external conditions than of governmental virtue. Economic progress had occurred *despite* the gross incompetence of the regime. Rightly or wrongly, it was argued that the gathering crisis that culminated in collapse of the system was due partly to lack of proper planning. Planning was the instrument advanced for overcoming the crisis facing the young democracy as its ultimate test of strength.[32]

THE MOMENT OF CRISIS

The fundamental crisis was one of frustration. The Venezuelan people had few genuine roots in the countryside. Like most other Latins, their orientation was predominantly to the city: they readily abandoned their farms in hope of participating in the larger society. A decade of rapid economic growth—the gross national product had doubled—and ostentatious living by a few had raised expectations to unreasonable heights. The ideology of a development society which was increasingly gaining acceptance reinforced existing values and created a sense of great urgency in solving the many distressing problems which, so it seemed to many, perversely prevented advance into the millenium of plenty, equality, and justice. Rural illiterates were inclined to be fatalistic, their philosophy born of prolonged misery and despair. But the new middle class, sensing its power, was growing restless and impatient. It sought to slice the Gordian knot, and by some sleight-of-hand, make problems vanish. A few hoped for an "enlightened" dictatorship that would quickly set the world aright. Others advocated a full-scale Marxist revolution as the "final" solution. Still others believed in the magical potency of "planning." Somehow, all problems were to be painlessly resolved by the chemistry of reason.

The crisis of frustration had two main aspects: the first was of a short-range nature and concerned the economic depression that had settled upon the country during 1958; the second involved more long-term considerations. The depression was tangible and unavoidable.

Income had ceased to grow, unemployment was spreading, capital was being expatriated in huge amounts. The so-called Emergency Plan was only a stop-gap measure that had no lasting effects. The economy stagnated four long years. Yet somehow the belief in planning was not shattered. On the contrary its prestige was enhanced each year. People were critical of the government for not doing more, but no one held planning responsible. Its magic might not be working as rapidly as had perhaps been hoped. But as part of a development ideology, it was nearly impervious to failure. Nationalism, economic development, and planning continued as the leading ideas throughout the period.

The second aspect of the crisis related to the prospects of reaching the long-term development goals which were in currency and about which there seemed little basic disagreement. But the depression, prolonged as it was over a period of years, put their attainment in doubt. At any rate, they were no longer seen as the inevitable future toward which the country would evolve. The immense structural problems of the economy would have to be tackled in a coordinated fashion, with priorities carefully worked out. This clearly called for the kind of technical expertise that only planning could provide.[33] Planning and development became irrevocably linked. As the crisis deepened, it also strengthened adherence to the development ideology as whose champion the new middle class leadership had proclaimed itself.

And so, paradoxically, national planning created its own conditions for survival. Intended as a crisis-relieving instrument, it also dramatized in "facts and figures" the continuing gap between aspirations and current conditions. But in this it succeeded only in stirring the crisis of frustration still further.

The birth of national planning in Venezuela under conditions of crisis had two immediate consequences. First, it put a high premium on its effectiveness. At the very least, this meant that government was willing to give active support to the establishment of a workable planning process and would make use of it in ways that seemed politically opportune. Second, it meant that short-term problems would be given priority attention. Long-range speculation on alternative goal possibilities is a luxury in which planners can indulge only when there are no problems of great urgency to be met or when planners forego whatever chances they may have found for influencing major decisions. A second paradox of planning, therefore, is this: When planning is least needed—as under conditions of relative calm and stability—it can afford to be "rational"; but when level-headed rationality is desperately wanted—as under pressure of an extreme crisis—planning is given the least scope for exercising its manifest function. More than ever, it becomes then an extension of politics, and planners find themselves rushing madly about putting out fires wherever they can. Such behavior, it is true, may well be considered appropriate to the circumstances, but its rationality is of an altogether different sort from the cool evaluation of alternatives and consequences normally associated with that concept.

This raises an interesting issue for planning theory. If the paradox stated holds true, planning typically occurs—and receives political backing—under conditions of crisis. The rationality of planning practice must therefore be a rationality adapted to its conditions: it must sacrifice comprehensiveness to the urgency of overcoming specific bottlenecks; it must be more problem- than goal-oriented; it must be piecemeal and fragmented rather than coordinative.[34] Unfortunately, many would-be planners regret this passing of functional rationality to the point where they fail to see the rationality in successfully adaptive behavior to crisis situations. According to their canons, the crisis should never have arisen; that it has is interpreted as a failure of planning, as the result of distorted, "irrational" behavior.

A planner adapted to crisis, however, might argue differently. Rather than avoid them, he might welcome crises and encourage them—though he would wish to hold them strictly within bounds, a feat not always easy to accomplish. For crises always occur when there is rapid change and this, of course, is precisely the condition of modern economic development. Crisis situations may stimulate rather than retard the pace of progress. Accordingly, the *real* national crisis in such countries as Venezuela would be the absence of one. This, at least, is the reading obtained from a philosophical position that accepts change as the *normal* condition of human enterprise and a static analytical framework as a radical departure from reality. Crisis-adapted rationality is consequently much closer to the normal climate of decision-making than is the formal means-ends schema proposed by economists and logicians.

Something like crisis planning has prevailed in Venezuela since CORDIPLAN's inception. Even the formal planning period was only four years, and most of the work in actual fact concentrated upon the annual budget and its accompanying program. As the director of national planning once remarked to this writer, 90 per cent of his staff time is spent on day-to-day problems. There is simply no time to look beyond four years into the future. And even this modest period will frequently seem irrelevant for decisions.[35]

III

The Evolution of Planning

THE SUCCESS OF NATIONAL PLANNING

Venezuela's experience with national planning can in many respects be called successful. With only minor exceptions, planning has become universally accepted by the more articulate sectors of public opinion as a process for promoting national development. An essentially skeptical, if not downright hostile, business community has been won over to the idea of national planning. Héctor Hurtado, who served as director of CORDIPLAN during 1963, summarized the new business philosophy at the Barcelona meeting of the Federation of Chambers of Commerce and Industry (Fedecámeras). Planning, he said, is now accepted by the business community as an adequate instrumentality of economic development. He called attention to certain statements in a document that had been approved by the meeting and in which the role of the state in planning was acknowledged and emphasized. But still more important, according to Hurtado, was the spreading recognition that economic development must not be carried out for the exclusive benefit of the entrepreneurial class alone or for any single group whatever but in the interest of all Venezuelans. The national interest had become dominant.[1] Among other things, the document to which Hurtado referred, "The General Bases of Venezuela's Economic Development," asserted that "the plan—if it is used as a basis for consultation with all qualified sectors—is the beginning of a rational and democratic planning of public expenditures."[2]

Since its inception, CORDIPLAN has enjoyed growing prestige and, as a result, must be reckoned with as a major force in the de-

31

cisions of government. It has been able to function well within the general provisions of its enabling legislation. A series of important planning documents have appeared, the latest of which is the *Plan de la Nación 1963–1966,* and targets as well as policies have been subjected to continuous review and to revision when the need arose. Understanding of the process of economic transformation in Venezuela and the intricate relationships of its manifold variables is now far superior to the knowledge existing at the beginning of the period of national planning. And this understanding has spread to wider and wider circles within the government no less than in the private sector, and has improved the quality of public discussion of economic questions. The plan itself has become a major focus of public interest.

CORDIPLAN has encouraged the establishment of new planning units, or the strengthening of already existing ones, in the various ministries and other public agencies. For their guidance it has begun to publish an annual "Operational Plan" that includes major policy guidelines for project programming. The program-budget has become reality. Though not a legally binding document, it is now submitted to the Congress as an annex to the annual fiscal budget. Since the two documents are quite differently structured, the program-budget has so far been of little help in the course of normal budgetary review. But during the presidential campaign, revision of the budgetary law to include the program-budget as the principal document for congressional action received support from all the major candidates.

The program-budget is drawn up by CORDIPLAN in close collaboration with the ministries and autonomous agencies. CORDIPLAN is also the home base for a large number of intergovernmental committees for achieving greater coordination of government policies and programs in certain critical areas such as industrialization, electrification, or community development. In this way planning reaches far down into the governmental hierarchy. But it also extends into the private sector. A permanent consultative commission to CORDIPLAN, composed of representatives from government, business, labor, and the Association of Economics, has been set up to advise on questions on national planning.[3] In short, CORDIPLAN has become effectively tied to the decision structure of the country. From being the exclusive function of a single agency, planning has spread to encompass all major decision points, with CORDIPLAN increasingly assuming the role of coordinator and mediator of conflicting interests. Above all, planning has succeeded in focusing attention on economic development as the principal project of government and, indeed, of the nation. Actions are no longer justified in the public view unless they contribute in some way to the development of the nation's capacities in the economic or cultural fields.

These are major accomplishments, widely acknowledged. Other successes are less well known, and not as readily apparent. Since a good part of this section is devoted to their identification, I shall pass on to a critical question concerning the effectiveness of national planning. Has it, in fact, led to the more rapid growth of the economy? Unfortunately, answers to this question must remain ambiguous. We do not know what economic performance would have been in the absence of planning. On the other hand, throughout the planning period, major economic targets for national product, unemployment, and sectoral performance have *not* been met. The depression that lasted from 1958 to 1961 was caused largely by exogenous forces which stubbornly resisted government efforts at internal recovery. The upturn in the economy during 1962 was again more the result of an improvement in the world markets for petroleum than of government policy. Whether this relative impotency of government to direct the economic fortunes of the nation will continue in the future remains an open question. In view of the repeated failure to achieve economic targets, the rising prestige of CORDIPLAN as an institution, and of national planning in a more general sense, is somewhat of a puzzle. Since goal attainment is among the manifest functions of planning, one is led to ask why national planning has been successful at all, even by the more unorthodox criteria enumerated above.

Three general explanations will be offered. The first is concerned with the institutional form of planning and the planners' own conception of their role. The second has to do with the shift that has occurred in moving from doctrinaire reasoning to a form of dialogue which converted the planning process into an effective instrument of conjunction. The third explanation looks for the hidden role of planning, its manifold "uses" that lie beyond functional rationality and goal achievement. In a certain sense the last two are more than explanations of successful planning; they are results of a particular conception of planning. Form and function cannot be separated here; a self-reinforcing process has been set into motion in which the results of planning strengthen its form, while its form insures a range of successful outcomes. In actuality the three-part explanation that will be given forms a web of cause-and-effect relations whose dissection into discrete elements is essentially arbitrary and serves a primarily didactic purpose.

AUTHORITY AND ROLE CONCEPTION

The basic reason for the success of national planning in Venezuela will be found in the manner in which it came to be integrated into the organizational structure of government. Planning succeeded because it could speak with the voice of authority and its role was accepted within the government hierarchy as a legitimate endeavor. How planning became authoritative will be discussed under institutional aspects; how it acquired legitimacy will be explained in terms of the self-conception that Venezuela's national planners had of their own role.

Institutional aspects

From the very beginning CORDIPLAN was housed in Miraflores, the presidential palace in Caracas. At first glance this seems incongruous. Miraflores is heavily guarded and physical access to it is, at best, difficult. Certainly CORDIPLAN is far less approachable than many other government offices. For an agency whose primary activity includes coordination, this seems an anomalous location, until one discovers that CORDIPLAN's authority derives in large measure from its propinquity to the president himself, its geographic position at the very apex of the national power pyramid. No other agency has an advantage similar to CORDIPLAN's of being within earshot of the president. Successful coordination in planning made this relationship even more important than any possible improvement in accessibility to government ministries or the public. CORDIPLAN partook of the president's authority and frequently spoke with his approval on controversial matters. CORDIPLAN instructions, emanating from Miraflores, had to be taken seriously by other agencies. No one could ignore or bypass the agency, unless he went directly to the president. But inasmuch as the president relied heavily on CORDIPLAN, any petition or proposal that had a bearing on the economy was eventually sent to CORDIPLAN for review and opinion.

The director of national planning has always been a man who enjoyed the close confidence of the president. Great personal prestige was an additional requirement for the job. For the planning director would attend meetings of the cabinet when economic matters were discussed and in other ways take part in high government councils. If he wished to influence decisions, he had to be widely respected as a person.

The first planning director, Manuel Pérez Guerrero, was an economist who was held in high regard even beyond the circles of his own political party. For a few months during 1948 he served as minister of finance in the newly elected government under Rómulo Gallegos. Subsequently, he went to work for the United Nations, where he soon attained high rank as an international civil servant. He was a man of mature judgment, cosmopolitan outlook, and public stature. The choice of Pérez Guerrero is interesting, since the leading and, in a sense, more obvious candidate for the office was Enrique Tejera Paris, who had headed the Preparatory Commission. But Tejera Paris was slated for other work. Awarded the governorship of Sucre, he was eventually appointed Ambassador to the United States.

In 1962, when Pérez Guerrero returned to his post with the United Nations, his place was taken by Héctor Hurtado, who had previously been the technical director of CORDIPLAN. It was perhaps a sign of the agency's maturity that promotion to this important and powerful position should have come from among its own staff. Hurtado was a lawyer; but, like his predecessor, he belonged to the inner circle of Rómulo Betancourt and the Democratic Action party. Moreover, he was a politician of consummate skill and was grounded in the technical aspects of planning. Hurtado continued and further developed a tradition established by Tejera Paris and Pérez Guerrero in the preceding years.

CORDIPLAN's authority remained unimpaired during the entire period of its operations, partly because it wisely exercised restraint on its ambitions. The total national planning staff, including secretaries and messengers, at no time exceeded forty, and its annual budget was only the equivalent of about one million dollars.[4] With only a single exception its activities were devoted to research, advice, policy formulation, and decision-making. The one action program in which CORDIPLAN became involved—somewhat contrary to its desires—was community development, and this only because community development was thought of, in the main, as a coordinative activity that would employ only a skeleton staff. Even so, this program was separated from the regular functions of CORDIPLAN and in no way impaired the image the agency wished to further of itself as a modest office with no intention whatsoever of using its considerable influence to build an administrative empire that might threaten the established ministries.

In all these respects CORDIPLAN reflected Tejera Paris' basic thinking on the prerequisites for effective central planning. Planning should be linked to the executive system; authority is necessary for its successful functioning; and its duties should be restricted to those of a general staff in the military: it should eschew direct responsibilities for action.[5]

Role conception

How planners conceive of their own position in the government is important to the way they are publicly received: with hostility, skepticism, or matter-of-factness. In Venezuela a good part of this self-conception was built into the institutional structure of planning, but much depended on how well the leading planners understood their role. Some characteristics of the planning function have already been discussed in connection with planning legislation and Tejera Paris' ECLA study. His influence in planning, as elsewhere, has predominated. But a few additional points need to be brought out.

CORDIPLAN was convinced that most of the planning work should be done by others, specifically by the operating ministries and action agencies. Its purpose here was to strengthen existing decision poles and to help improve sectoral or partial planning, by training specialists in programming, providing a common framework of assumptions, and encouraging frequent exchange of information and ideas.

In an early speech Tejera Paris had clearly stated the basic philosophy.

The first principle, then, of the national system—of our system of planning, which is not copied but uniquely Venezuelan—does not consist in the creation of a vast central institution. It is rather the establishment of a national system which embraces all efforts of public administration as well as related actions of the private sector. And instead of being imposed from the top, planning draws its inspiration from a common policy or doctrine, a common body of knowledge, common objectives, a personal relationship among the planners, and a great Venezuelan feeling of cordiality. For this reason the system has quickly taken root. . . .

Until recently each ministry was planning only for itself, in the hope, nearly always frustrated, that its efforts would be rewarded with a larger share of the national budget.

We, today, believe in a very small system of coordination which will maintain direct relations with all the planning and implementing offices of government. And this small central office has as its principal object the guidance and coordination of all their efforts.[6]

The coordinative function was thus emphasized, but informal methods were preferred to more formal obligations. There was no thought of creating an abstract planning system in which all parts would neatly mesh on flow charts to culminate in a national plan. On the contrary, personal relations were stressed, and a good deal of the coordination occurred in *ad hoc* or standing committees brought together by CORDIPLAN, which also provided the administrative overhead for committees of this sort. In a governmental system such as Venezuela's, where ministerial secrecy was an accepted pattern of public performance, these committees served a useful role in permitting information to pass among the interested parties to a policy or a decision. The system was by no means perfect, and some ministries, agriculture for example, have been unwilling to participate in these and similar coordinative efforts. A word from the president, or the removal of a minister, might have brought results more quickly and virtually imposed coordination as a requirement upon all the ministries. But this line of action was wisely avoided. CORDIPLAN opted for a course of least resistance, stressing the voluntary character of coordinative efforts. And by thus avoiding a direct assault upon the ministerial power structure, it also gained ready acceptance, or at least tolerance, for its work. This was an important gain.

CORDIPLAN also operated on the assumption that, in order to get its work done, only minimal public consensus was required. Communists and priests will join to build a schoolhouse for their village. The same principle was invoked at the national level. CORDIPLAN tended to avoid discussions of principle and preferred to work within the context of realistic alternatives. Its search was for what Uslar Pietri has called the "possible" Venezuela. Hence, a short-time horizon was consistently stressed. Lengthy discussions of development objectives were avoided; the immediate needs, such as massive unemployment or industrial diversification, were sufficiently clear and understood. In the latest version of the four-year national plan, for instance, there is only the sketchiest mention of general goals in a reference to the statement drafted in May 1962 which has been cited earlier.[7] Few flights of philosophical fancy were permitted, and always the planning text returns to a concrete setting, replete with data and analysis.

It may be appropriate here briefly to describe the substance of the plan itself. In view of the paucity of trustworthy information, it was rather sophisticated in its methodology. The general frame of reference was set by a series of "balances" between the demand and supply of labor, consumption and investment, payments and receipts of foreign exchange, directly productive and social investment, private and public sectors, and so forth. The growth rate in the national product was accepted as a key variable and set at 7.9 per cent per annum for the period 1962 to 1966; but the principal objective was, for obvious political reasons, the reduction of urban unemployment.

The plan was presented essentially as a four-year program; a set of projections to 1975 was formally included, but little significance was attached to it. In spite of this short time horizon, however, the plan was seriously deficient in functionally relating project planning to sectoral programs, and these, in turn, to a specific geographic context. The planning process in Venezuela has not yet advanced far enough to achieve the perfect coordination of project, program, and plan for sectors and regions that many economists expect of it. With respect to the private sector, the plan was at best "indicative" in the French manner, though as late as May 1963 private enterprise had not yet been extensively consulted. The plan was instead concerned predominantly with setting formal production, employment, and investment targets, often in appreciable detail. Its sectoral "plans," for the most part, represented summaries of agency programs that had frequently not been formally coordinated or subjected to an intensive review process by CORDIPLAN. Some discussion of what was called "instrumentation" was, however, included and referred to statements of basic policy which emerged from a consideration of the general planning framework.

These comments scarcely do justice to a document that provides a basis for policy and program decisions few other countries can boast. Not the least of its virtues derives from the fact that it is treated as a working document, subject to frequent modification. Annual planning reports supplement the larger document and give it the historical relevance it might otherwise have lacked. Every two years fundamental revision of the plan is undertaken, with projections for another four-year period. Serving mainly as a discussion document, the plan has no legal force whatever. The only portion voted upon is the fiscal budget accompanied by a program detailing its physical components.

The plan, in short, is somewhat like a drifting cloud. Its very appearance in a loose-leaf binding is ephemeral. But if policies, programs, and projects may be changed from year to year, if CORDIPLAN will lean over backwards to accommodate, say, business or farming interests in the plan, what is left of the central planning function? What is left, of course, is a process of quite responsible decision-making which has the benefit of a forward look and a comprehensive analysis of the economy's problems, stressing the interdependency of phenomena. What the plan contains, by way of substance, is only secondary to the process of plan formulation. It is treated not as an inviolable document, a bible, but as a temporary summing-up of current knowledge, expectations, and desirabilities. It took a long time for this concept to filter down and pass into general knowledge, and even now it is doubtful how far it has been accepted. But it has certainly helped to shape the attitudes of CORDIPLAN officials themselves, encouraging them to build communication bridges to all major decision poles. Dogmatism has been eschewed. The great virtues of planning have been its tolerance and patience. Potential opponents found themselves in a quandary, attacking an enemy that would recede at every charge. But this strategy was played from strength, not weakness. The substance was not sacrificed. It was the data that were resilient to doctrinal fumings. Planning helped to uncover them, and planners as well as others would have to come to terms with them. The means might be compromised, but the long-range goals of a development society could not. And on these goals there was little fundamental disagreement.

A New Mentality

Contrary to CORDIPLAN's conception, the national plan was by many regarded as the official government "doctrine" or, as we would call it, the party line. And of doctrines in Venezuela there was, indeed, no shortage. Almost belligerently, doctrines and manifestos were put forward by any group aspiring to public standing. They usually fell into the same pattern: a lengthy analysis of what was called the reality of Venezuela was followed by solutions which, more or less badly, fitted that conception. Every group would, of course, have its own version of what was "real" and would, if anything, emphasize those aspects of its doctrine that would distinguish it from every other. Originality and a flair for expression were valued nearly as much as analytical depth. The First National Convention of Economists, for instance, produced a document entitled *Diagnosis of the National Economy,* whose 208 pages were typical of the sort of rhetoric in common use. The convention was held in May 1963. It is telling that conservative economists had withdrawn prior to the convention—on ideological grounds, of course. This left the Marxists and their sympathizers more or less in control of the situation. A quote from the introduction, as it appeared in a one-page spread in the respected newspaper, *El Nacional,* will give the flavor of the sort of reasoning that pitted group against group, plan against plan.

> Analysis of the materials presented to the convention with respect to the origin and perspectives of the current crisis which holds the country in its grip, permits one to arrive at the following conclusions:
>
> One: that said crisis is the crisis of the existing economic structure of the country.
>
> Two: that this structure is the historical result of the inser-

tion of the petroleum and mining sector into the backward, traditional structure of Venezuela and its subsequent evolution in time.[8]

A year earlier, Fedecámeras had produced a similar type of statement, the "Economic Charter of Mérida," which was called "a program for the orientation of national development . . . the fundamental economic thesis of the Federation regarding the efficient solution of our present economic and social problems." [9] And so it went with almost every organization. Even distant ECLA, the United Nations Economic Commission with headquarters in Chile, was given to pronouncements of this sort.

It was, therefore, only reasonable that the national plan should be regarded as simply one of a large number of competing doctrinal positions. This image, of course, could easily become disastrous to national planning. It would prevent a dialogue, with opposing sides talking *past,* not *at,* each other. If planning were to become the basis for a national effort at development, the image of the plan as doctrine had to be wiped out. But the demands of planning went even further. In national planning there was to be no room for doctrinal thinking of any sort, and past habits of thought would have to be abandoned for a more flexible give-and-take of mutual accommodation.

The key group here was what is euphemistically called the business community. Without its active participation, plan targets and policies were not likely to be attained. Peasant and labor organizations were politically "safe" and could be more or less relied upon to go along with national programs. But many businessmen were suspicious of government intentions to the point of hostility.

So long as government confined itself to servicing their immediate interests—such as establishing protective tariffs, or paying production subsidies—there was no general outcry against governmental "interference and planning." The red flag was hoisted rather at the inclusion of planning in a development ideology where it seemed to convey the meaning of a centrally directed socialist economy. The main issue of contention was the extent to which government should become involved in the areas of decision-making reserved by tradition to the private sector. The issue is well known and much belabored. But in most parts of the world, the fighting slogans—Road to Serfdom, Planning or Freedom—have a decidedly dated sound.[10] It was perhaps inevitable that sides would form once more on Venezuelan ground.

The business community itself was divided on the question, and the two opposing sides were locked in a bitter struggle for control of the powerful Federation of Chambers of Commerce and Industry. Dichotomies are dangerous simplifications, and in this case the concept fails to do justice to the complexity of ideological positions of business leaders and their following. A close study of the evolution of business attitudes would show a kaleidoscope of shifting alliances for the period 1958–1963. Nevertheless, without excessive violence to known facts, it is possible to describe the ideological division that had occurred in terms of a conservative-progressive polarity.

Members of the old and discredited oligarchy were among the leaders of the conservative wing: Nicomedes Zuloaga, hijo, Armando Espinosa, Oscar Machado Zuloaga. Representing primarily the large commercial and financial interests centered in Caracas, they had become the great champions of free enterprise. Their contemporary hero was the genial Ludwig Erhard, whose updated Manchester liberalism was widely credited with the "miracle" of postwar German recovery. Conservative business groups remained without organizational backbone until 1962, when the Independent Venezuelan Association (AVI) was founded, evidently to exert influence on the national elections scheduled for the following year. AVI did not claim to be a political party as such, although it frequently behaved as one. It was financially powerful and basically distrusted the "New Dealish" philosophies espoused by the major competing parties, including Democratic Action. However, it did not present a completely unified front, even under pressure of the shortly forthcoming elections, and a "Liberal" wing within AVI exerted a moderating influence on many of its policies.

The "progressives" tended to coalesce around another so-called nonpolitical organization, Pro-Venezuela, which had been founded in 1958.[11] Comparisons are frequently misleading, but it may help to suggest that Pro-Venezuela was in many respects similar to Americans for Democratic Action in the United States. Basically, the organization was sympathetic to the government, although it maintained a public stance of nonpartisanship. Its membership was much more broadly based than that of AVI, including on its National Council most of the important organized interest groups in the country: the Church, professional associations, the universities, the military, newspapers, and women's groups. But businessmen predominated, not only in its membership but in financial support as well. Pro-Venezuela spoke chiefly for the new industrialists, commercial farmers, and small merchants throughout the country. In contrast to AVI, its position was more "nationalistic," and among its primary goals was the rapid industrialization of Venezuela's economy. "Buy Venezuelan" was one of its favorite slogans.

Significantly, the progressives derived their main strength from provincial areas, such as Aragua, Carabobo, Lara, Portuguesa, Zulia, and Anzoátegui, while the conservative stronghold remained in Caracas. It is worth noting in this connection that the Democratic Action party had its poorest showing during both the 1958 and 1963 elections in the national capital where it obtained only 15 per cent of the popular vote. The main support for Venezuela's social revolution came from the "periphery." [12]

This alignment of interest reflected the changing character of Venezuela's economy: its industrialization, the incorporation of the provinces in the economic life of the nation, the critical importance of government in economic development, the need for a protective nationalistic policy during the period of economic transition, the increasing interdependency of economic institutions. The progressives were clearly riding the "wave of history," and the outcome of the conflict was fairly predictable. The basic lines of division are shown in schematic form below.

	CONSERVATIVES	PROGRESSIVES
Sectors:	Large commerce (especially in export-import lines) and banking-finance	Industry, commercial farming, small- and medium-scale business enterprise
Geographic focus:	Caracas	Provinces
Doctrine:	Free enterprise; anti-planning; antigovernment	Recognition of the role of the state in economic life; acceptance of indicative planning; progovernment
Nationalism:	Weak	Strong
Organizational focus:	Independent Venezuelan Association (AVI), after 1962	Pro-Venezuela, after 1958

The battle was joined in Fedecámeras, over which the old guard had succeeded in gaining a measure of control. As a result, the organization was excluded from further participating in the National Council of Pro-Venezuela. That was in 1960. Its final defeat in the leadership of Fedecámeras did not come until three years later. By then its basic strategy had been eroded by the changing political tides in the country.

The conservative business group had wanted a government that, as in the days of old, would be run in their exclusive interest. For some years subsequent to the 1958 uprising, it must have harbored some hope that the military would again intercede and dispose of a regime whose ideology and policies it loathed. But if such hopes were ever entertained—and the evidence is purely inferential—they must have been dashed in April 1960 when an attempted coup under old-guard General Castro Leoni failed utterly in gaining popular support. When two subsequent military uprisings were similarly crushed, the waning power of the armed forces to impose their political will had become plain to everyone. The clock of history could no longer be turned back.

In the meantime the direct threat of Communism was growing. President Betancourt's uncompromising opposition to this threat strengthened his hand against the remnants of the former oligarchy. A more conciliatory, neutralist posture on his part would have played into their hands. But through matchless political skill he succeeded both in containing Communist terrorism and in reducing what remained of the oligarchy to almost total impotence.

At the 1962 meeting of Fedecámeras, the struggle for leadership between the conservative and progressive factions flared into the open, but the former still managed to maintain its position. A basic policy statement, "The Economic Charter of Mérida," was produced outlining Fedecámera's views on the role of private enterprise in a developing economy. Its tone was doctrinaire and left no opening for conversations with the government. But a close reading of the text shows it as a lucid, reasonable statement. On specific subjects it diverged sharply from existing government policies—the sensitive petroleum policy is a case in point—but on the whole it was far less to the "right" than might have been expected. Concrete references to planning were, on the whole, avoided, except for a statement that planning for the government's "own activities" was legitimate. What this meant, however, was not entirely clear when

45 per cent of the total investment effort was financed from the public treasury. Elsewhere in the Charter of Mérida there was frequent mention of development goals, the need to subordinate all efforts to this common imperative, the necessity for achieving a comprehensive and integral vision of the development process, and similar expressions that suggested national planning without actually mentioning it.[13] The charter undoubtedly represented a compromise between the two major factions vying for control in Fedecámeras. Its reputation as a "reactionary" doctrine is therefore somewhat surprising.

In any event, the internal struggle for power was resolved in favor of the "progressive" forces by the time the next annual meeting was held in the provincial capital of Barcelona. CORDIPLAN, which had been rebuffed the previous year, was this time present in full force. Héctor Hurtado, as CORDIPLAN's director, took part in many phases of the program, reviewing and commenting on a number of position papers and explaining the purpose of national planning to whoever was willing to listen. In a strategic move, he proposed the creation of a permanent consultative commission which would give the businessman an effective voice in national planning.

Two main propositions were warring for support.[14] According to the first, the existing national plan was wholly unacceptable and was to be replaced by one which would, in effect, be drafted by Fedecámeras itself. This point of view was supported by the conservative wing but failed to gain general concurrence. The second proposition admitted the existence of certain positive features in the plan and went along with CORDIPLAN's intention of revising it on the basis of consultations with business and other private sectors. This was the "progressive" position and it carried the day. The meeting closed on a note of great cordiality. Hurtado praised the "forward-looking" spirit of Fedecámeras and, in his concluding speech, President Betancourt announced the creation of a consultative commission.

The Barcelona meeting seemed to many to have ushered in a new era. Luis Vallenilla, President of the Venezuelan Development Corporation (CVF), took the occasion to speak of the "new managerial attitude." In a speech scarcely a fortnight later, he declared:

> Businessmen have decided on a far-reaching collaboration with the state. . . . One might say that the grave reservations which

previously existed concerning the planning functions of the state have largely disappeared. The negative attitude with regard to public investment projects has been abandoned. In this new position, management becomes associated with and runs risks even in projects and programs which have their origin in government memoranda.[15]

As examples, Vallenilla cited mixed public-private financing of industrial projects; the creation by private capital of a mortgage-financing institution that would fulfill essentially a public function by helping to stabilize the mortgage market; and the creation, with assistance from the World Bank, of a private development financing corporation.

Only the last two were recent accomplishments, and even they had been in progress for some time. But Vallenilla's speech was intended to reinforce the new climate of conciliation and cooperation. It is also not without interest that Fedecámeras was readmitted to the National Council of Pro-Venezuela shortly after the Barcelona conference.

A leading member of Fedecámeras, Luis Fernando Yepez, gave succinct expression to the new spirit. In a signed article entitled "Fedecámeras and the National Plan," he wrote:

It is both just and necessary to emphasize . . . the intelligent spirit of tolerance which was demonstrated by the government's representatives. A consultative commission, such as the one proposed by Hurtado and announced by President Betancourt, could be of incalculable benefit to the country, especially at the present moment. If it is well put together, with business, labor, and the democratic parties—those in power as well as of the opposition—being represented, the commission could (1) be converted into a forum for the discussion of the country's fundamental problems which, because of excessive political pugnacity, are today relegated to a secondary place; (2) extract development plans from the shifting conveniences and contingencies of politics; (3) contribute to creating a national conscience with respect to the necessity of economic development and encourage the collective commitment required by this task; and (4) demonstrate that—despite the superficial embellishments of polemical rhetoric—there exists in the country an almost complete consensus on what has to be done and what the nation is asking with pressing urgency of the present Venezuelan generation.

This last point I consider fundamental. I am convinced that for the great majority of Venezuelans our economic development and our political democracy are not so much questions of doctrine as problems of efficient work and good administration.[16]

Yepez' optimism was nothing new, however. It echoed sentiments that had for years been expressed by Pro-Venezuela in its public pronouncements. Its significance was that it reflected the changing balance of forces within Fedecámeras. The progressive faction, symbolizing the rising power of the "periphery" over the "center," had moved into control.[17]

THE USES OF PLANNING

In discussing this topic, an important distinction must be drawn between what may be called the manifest and latent functions of planning.[18] By the former are meant both the pattern of expected performance and the intended "contribution" of planning to a social project such as economic development, city-building, or industrial production. The second describes the unintended, subtle contributions of planning to the social order.

Planning was introduced to Venezuela primarily for the manifest functions commonly associated with it. A search of the theoretical literature on planning reveals the recurrence of a few basic themes which adumbrate its central meaning.

Planning is more and more regarded as equivalent to rational social action, that is, as a social process for reaching a rational decision.[19]

Planning is the process of preparing a set of decisions for action in the future, directed at achieving goals by optimal means.[20]

Planning is the rational application of knowledge to the process of making decisions which will serve as a basis for human action.[21]

These definitions are fairly standard, and they raise expectations about certain performance characteristics attributed to planning. Thus, planning is nearly always characterized by its functionally rational approach to decision-making. For a given set of ends, planners are expected to review realistic alternative means for attaining them, study the probable consequences of each, and present their conclusions to a political decision-making body for consideration. This approach does not exclude the possibility of clarifying the meaning of the ends (or value premises) which are generated through the political process, nor the possible task of reducing general objectives to more specific targets, projects, and programs.

The study of means-ends chains is a technical assignment which may bring into play a variety of scientific methods of analysis. Most people, including many planners, tend to think of this analysis, which they regard as the hard core of planning practice, as a purely objective function. Planning is consequently presented as a morally neutral activity that in no way involves the values of the planners themselves. Planners prepare decisions; they do not make them. According to the Interamerican Society of Planning, "to the extent that planning refers to the rational quality of decisions for action, it is inherent in such decisions and therefore independent of values which motivate action and determine the nature of objectives." [22] And again: "The 'decision to plan' is an abbreviated expression of 'the decision to base decisions which lead to action on a satisfactory knowledge of reality.' " [23] Scientific knowledge, objectivity, moral neutrality, instrumental rationality—all these terms enter into the public image of planning. They are part of its expected role performance.

National economic planning, specifically, was further expected to lead to speedy and efficient achievement of the developmental goals of the country. Efficiency, in the sense of reduction of waste resulting from inappropriate and inadequately coordinated policies, was here the main consideration. Planners were to be concerned with the optimal pattern of resource allocation for given long-range purposes. In Venezuela's case these included rapid growth of production, full employment, industrial diversification, and the like.

If judged by these standards, and especially by its contribution to economic development, national planning in Venezuela was not unambiguously successful. Key short-term objectives were not being achieved. Whether substantial efficiencies were obtained from planning is difficult to ascertain, but very likely its contribution here was only of minor importance. And if specific policy decisions are viewed under the microscope, the influence of instrumental rationality appears very small, indeed, in most instances.[24] Other studies of planning have arrived at essentially similar conclusions.[25] It would seem that the popular image of planning has only the most tenuous of relations to reality.

But if so, how is one to explain the rising prestige of national planning in Venezuela? This question leads to a consideration of the latent functions of national planning. There must have been positive contributions of planning to the social system other than those which may be subsumed under the concept of rationality. The question is of key importance not only with regard to Venezuela's experience but, more generally, for planning theory. It poses further critical questions such as the relation of latent functions to the structure of the planning process and the relation of manifest to latent functions in planning. Answers will have far-reaching implications for the practice of planning and for a proper conceptualization of the planner's role in society.

The latent functions of national planning in Venezuela will be discussed under five subject headings: strengthening the presidency; improving the political process; creating a development society; reducing social conflict; and mobilizing additional resources. They are called latent here because they normally pass unmentioned in any discussion of the purposes of planning. This does not mean that those who devised Venezuela's planning structure were entirely unaware of the possible social role of planning; indeed, there are contrary indications. Most technicians both inside and outside CORDIPLAN nevertheless continue to rest their evaluation of the effectiveness of planning primarily on its function in improving critical means-ends relationships and, more specifically, on the ability of planning to "generate" a sufficiently high rate of economic growth and a substantial reduction of unemployment. As will be seen, however, the question may legitimately be raised whether the latent functions of planning were not, on balance, more important to the development of Venezuela as a modern democratic nation.

Strengthening the presidency

National planning was of immense value to the president himself. He could rely on CORDIPLAN for confidential, trustworthy, and
expert advice on economic questions, advice that was at the same
time independent of vested interests in any ongoing program. This
improved his own judgment and facilitated the shaping of consistent
policies and the over-all coordination of government programs.
Where the president would have been more or less dependent on
the opinions of his ministers, each representing only a single group
of related program-interests, he was now able clearly to assert a
national interest in policy questions, with the backing of factual
and reasonably objective information.

This was no mean advantage. But even more important was the
flexibility and freedom of action he gained as a result of having
CORDIPLAN within reach. It relieved him of a good deal of the
political pressure that was directed at his office. For he was now in a
position to deflect petitions and requests for special consideration to
CORDIPLAN and its numerous working groups. As a result, he might
never need to act upon them or, if an issue were of sufficient importance, take it under advisement only after an extensive inter-
ministerial review of it had been made.

An example will help to clarify the point. A group of physicians
who enjoyed direct access to the president had approached him at
one point with a request for authorizing the construction of a vast
cardiological institute in Caracas: a multistoried structure, the very
latest equipment, the usual seat of empire. The physicians, who
maintained close contact with Democratic Action, could not easily
be refused. But they were told that while the president himself was
in sympathy with their request, a small formality required that the
project first be reviewed by CORDIPLAN and its committee on public
health. Since the concept of planning had been legitimated, there
was little the physicians could do but take their request to CORDI-
PLAN. The outcome of this story is typical of many similar instances.
In reviewing the proposal, it was found that cardiological research
could easily be incorporated into a hospital project being considered
for early construction in Caracas. Only small adjustments were
needed to include in the projected hospital a *section* devoted to

cardiological research. The original proposal was thus drastically scaled down from its former size, but the compromise solution was nonetheless acceptable to the doctors. The hospital project was approved by CORDIPLAN; the physicians were satisfied to have got at least part of what they wanted; the president's political prestige remained unimpaired; and the nation as a whole had saved a significant amount in capital and foreign exchange.[26]

This story points to yet another function of planning, that of finding the most expeditious, least-cost solution to unavoidable political commitments. Two instances may be briefly cited. The first has to do with the claims of Ciudad Bolívar, capital of Bolívar state. For years enormous government investments had poured into the construction of a new industrial city some sixty miles away, and Ciudad Bolívar was now demanding "compensatory" attention. From a political standpoint, these demands had to be met; the only question was the form the investment should take. CORDIPLAN supported a project for construction of a bridge across the Orinoco River that would link both Ciudad Bolívar and the new city of Santo Tomé de Guayana with population centers to the north. This was a technically sound proposal that could be justified on broad policy considerations and offered a solution to the political problem that was defensible from a development standpoint.

The second example relates to a proposed railroad in the eastern provinces. Strong, if somewhat disorganized, political pressures were brought to bear on the administration for the approval of this costly and, it seemed to CORDIPLAN, uneconomic venture. But the project could not be included in the program budget without prior CORDIPLAN approval, while the president could always procrastinate by pointing out the need for further study. As a result, the project has been "held up" in CORDIPLAN for years, while alternative transportation plans were explored. Eventually, alternative transportation means may satisfy many of the present proponents of the project.

These are clear gains and important to the use of presidential powers. But perhaps the most important contribution, as far as the presidency is concerned, lies in the making of the national plan itself. As has been noted previously, this document serves chiefly as a basis for government-wide policy discussions and, in the future, may lead to an integration of private with public planning. But the plan nevertheless exists and stands as a symbol of government intentions. If plan targets are fulfilled, the president can then point with pride to the results; if they fail to be met, the plan may still be used to motivate more dedicated performance throughout the economy. The president may at any time invoke the symbolic power of the plan, underscoring intention rather than achievement, and counter criticism of government policies by reference to optimistic targets. Recent presidential messages have, in fact, stressed the central importance of the plan and references to it have been used to demonstrate the existence of intense government concern with leading problems, such as unemployment.

Improving the political process

Political behavior is improved whenever decisions are made more "responsible" by introducing technical reasoning. This may eliminate some problems from political consideration altogether, if objective criteria can be applied unambiguously and there is widespread consensus on the ends to be pursued. Alternatively, planning may serve as a constraint on political decision-making.

The point should not be belabored in the absence of detailed information on major policy decisions, but it seems clear, at least on a priori grounds, that the information generated by Venezuela's national system of planning must have had precisely this disciplinary effect on political debate. No one in the government, outside of CORDIPLAN itself, was responsible for keeping watch over the principal parameters of economic life, the total and sectoral growth rates, unemployment, balance of payments, and intersectoral and interregional balances. The basic data on performance might be collected and even analyzed elsewhere, at the Central Bank for instance. But no other agency related these data to developmental policy in the perspective of systematic projections of the economy.

These projections clearly revealed the limits of the possible. One could neither ignore nor arbitrarily reject them. Alternative projection models might be tested, but the frame of reference would remain constant. The national plan was the principal taskmaster in this endeavor. In many respects it was no more than a hypothesis for discussion, subject to continuous revision. But one could not tamper with any of its elements without affecting the total system of projections and plan targets. The quantitative rigor of its econometric models discouraged, even if it did not eliminate, irresponsible rhetoric. It forced the protagonists to fall back on reasoned arguments and think of incremental improvements in the plan itself rather than of grandiose schemes that would fail to meet the critical tests of consistency.

Creating a development society

National planning has helped to create a "new mentality." This was cited as its major achievement by the director of CORDIPLAN. He intended this to mean widespread acceptance of planning as a legitimate process of governmental decision-making and of the government's role in promoting economic development; acceptance by large segments of the public of national development objectives as significant points of reference for individual and group action; growing preference for technical-objective over ideological-doctrinal reasoning; and spreading practice of collaboration in a general planning process focusing on CORDIPLAN. Venezuela was becoming future-oriented and development-minded. Although this effect cannot be wholly attributed to the existence of national planning, as noted in earlier chapters, the observed changes would probably have been far less striking without it.

National goals were turned into powerful symbols of progress. They helped to draw the nation together in what Luis Fernando Yepez called the "supreme effort" of Venezuela's present generation. They stimulated new ideas and action. They helped to return discussion, whenever it strayed, to the basic theme. Whether the goals were being achieved was secondary to the effect they had on motivations. The same results might have been obtained without planning. But the existence of national planning meant that goals were presented as realistic opportunities set in the context of history rather than in some transhistorical utopia.

Planning acted as a countervailing force to a fatalism born of recurrent failure, poverty, and despair. It helped to create confidence in the possibilities of Venezuela's development and hope in the future of the nation. The rigorous means-ends logic of the plan suggested that even difficult problems were potentially capable of solution. The plan concretely embodied the aspirations of most Venezuelans and pointed to ways in which these aspirations might

grow into existential reality. Radical movements and sporadic violence were not only contained but pushed beyond the pale of public
approval. In a preelection dispatch from Caracas, the *New York
Times* Latin America correspondent, Tad Szulc, reported:

> Despite the daily violence and the promise of more to
> come, . . . the consensus in Venezuela is that the terrorist
> campaign has started to decline, having failed to win its politi-
> cal objectives. The Communist and extreme leftist leadership
> is said to face an urgent need to review basic strategy.
>
> The long and increasingly violent campaign has not only
> failed to win popular feeling against the Government but has
> also demonstrated that what the Marxists call "objective con-
> ditions" for a revolutionary seizure of power, do not exist in
> this country.[27]

The great majority of Venezuelans have come to trust in their power
for peaceful self-transformation.

Reducing social conflict

The plan has come to serve as an instrument for reconciling
competing interests into an image of the *national* interest which
would, in turn, exert influence on further decision-making. Planning
appears to have prevented a polarization of social forces into ideologically extreme positions—a danger that had been particularly
acute in Venezuela—and to have laid the basis for gradual expansion of the middle class by active recruitment from social orders in
the lower rungs of the hierarchy.[28]

Mobilizing external resources

In recent years the Alliance for Progress has made the existence
of national plans a virtual condition of external assistance. This aspect did not pass unnoticed in Venezuela. President Betancourt
declared:

> In addition to being necessary for the country, this plan also
> fulfills an international commitment to which Venezuela be-
> came party at the Punta del Este Conference in which the Al-
> liance for Progress . . . was approved.[29]

The presence of technically competent planning in Venezuela not only facilitated the work of the IBRD Mission to that country but was instrumental in obtaining the bank's approval of the gigantic Guri hyrdoelectric project that was to support the country's drive for industrialization.[30] In Venezuela resource mobilization was not a major reason for engaging in planning, but it contributed to its maintenance.

MANIFEST AND LATENT FUNCTIONS
IN NATIONAL PLANNING

This review of the major latent functions of national planning in Venezuela—its hidden consequences for social structure and process—points to an important conclusion: *The institutional form of national planning was essential to its popular success and contributed in a large way to the stability of democratic government over the last five years.*

This may be demonstrated by performing a simple mental experiment. We may ask what would have been the consequences of adopting a process-form of national planning that had the following characteristics relative to the system in use: more centralized; more authoritarian; more doctrinaire; more plan-oriented; more long-range; more exclusively "professional"; and more class-bound. The answer is more or less self-evident. Few, if any, of the latent functions described would have been performed. And if planning had failed both in this and in its manifest role, the entire enterprise of a development society under democratic leadership would have been endangered. Political instability would have threatened collapse of a pragmatic center and would have pushed the country to the brink of civil war. The situation would not have been unlike that which prevails in Brazil, a country that has attained a comparable degree of economic development but has so far failed to initiate a successful national planning process. In Brazil both right- and left-wing forces have gained at the expense of the center, leaving the government without the power to act decisively on major issues of social reform. It would be rash to blame all of Brazil's recent difficulties on a lack of effective national planning, but its absence almost certainly contributed to the growing social tensions within the country. National planning, if properly used, can be a powerful tool for achieving a working social balance.

National planning in Venezuela was not, however, instituted primarily for the latent functions it might perform. On the contrary, the set of consequences that have been described by this term came about as the by-product of an activity which is widely regarded as an effective method for improving the rationality of economic decisions and enhancing the prospects of economic growth. The élan of Venezuelan planning originally derived from popular expectations about its performance; clearly it was established for the sake of its *manifest* role. It follows that the far-reaching effects of planning described must be regarded as the direct outcome of an attempt to introduce functional rationality into the social decision process. To put it more radically, planning ideology was used by perceptive leaders, such as President Betancourt, Tejera Paris, Pérez Guerrero, and Héctor Hurtado, as a lever for achieving results which for both the public and many technical planners remained largely invisible. The stress placed on the manifest role of planning in the beginning was therefore necessary to insure the legitimacy and general acceptance of planning as a process.[31]

This early and strong indentification of planning in the public mind with functionally rational behavior naturally led to false expectations. Regardless of what the plan might stipulate, the economy seemed to go its own way, and it was often hard to tell whether even major government decisions were more functionally rational *with* planning than they might have been without it. And yet the prestige of planning rose. It did so, I have argued, because of the other consequences of planning which, though poorly understood, nevertheless helped to sustain it. But many of the latent consequences of planning would not have occurred if the model of functional rationality had been faithfully adhered to. The relative success of planning in Venezuela is the result not of functional but of adaptive rationality, that is, of rationality adapted to continuing crisis situations.

Creating a Development Society: The Case of Regional Planning

EMERGENCE OF THE REGIONAL ISSUE

The relation of regional to national planning has arisen as one of the key political—and policy—issues in Venezuela. The country's experience is not unique in this regard but is shared by many transitional societies whose economies are still imperfectly integrated in geographic space. Development occurs unequally among areas; vast geographic shifts in the structure of production and settlement accompany the processes of economic transformation. One result of these changes is mounting political pressures on the central government in support of regional planning. Because it is viewed as instrumental to development, and nonplanned change tends to exaggerate rather than attenuate interregional imbalances, planning is advocated as a solution for regional as well as national development problems. From a national standpoint, however, the question resolves into finding an adequate institutional form which will permit subordination of regional to national goals and formulating a policy for the geographic allocation of investment funds that will successfully combine economic growth criteria with those of equity in welfare and nudge the nation toward fuller integration in its spatial dimension.

The final part of Venezuela's national plan is devoted to questions of regional planning. But it accomplishes little beyond recognizing the existence of the problem and providing brief summaries of recent studies and ongoing programs with a regional focus. *No general policy for national development in its regional aspects is*

57

stated. As a result, the clash of conflicting interests continues un-abated. Only one thing is certain. Whether planned or not, some form of regional development on the country's economic periphery is bound to occur during the next generation. The country will not remain concentrated exclusively upon Caracas. Subsidiary centers will be strengthened. And some form of interregional integration will be the outcome of successful economic development at the na-tional level.

The regional issue was not posed in politically relevant terms until after the 1958 revolution. A definite center-periphery structure had by then emerged. The "center" was identified with Caracas and a number of near-by cities in the Valencia Basin which were draw-ing unto themselves a large share of the country's wealth and an in-creasing proportion of the total population. To support develop-ments at the center, regions peripheral to it were drained of much of their capital, manpower, and leadership. Except for investments in the oil industry in a few places, the peripheral economy was al-most totally neglected.[1]

Prolongation of this situation was bound to lead to conflict. Despite extensive migration to the center, the periphery still ac-counted for a majority of population in the country. Politically, this was significant. Moreover, some of the states, for instance Táchira and Zulia, were known for their proud regionalist traditions and their fierce loyalties to place. Where one was born and reared was not a negligible factor. Yet emotional regionalism found no satisfac-tory outlet. Local governments, for example, were almost totally de-pendent, financially as well as administratively, on Caracas. And they remained all but impotent to act in the interests of local pop-ulations.[2]

During the dictatorship states had lacked the means to exert effective political pressure on the central government for recogni-tion of their claims. The state governor was an agent of the president, and Venezuela's dictator-presidents had no need to justify their actions to the people. After 1958, however, this situation changed.[3] The government had been elected by the provincial vote. If it failed to make its appeal there, the opposition would automatically be strengthened. It is therefore scarcely accidental that industrial diver-sification and decentralization appeared among the primary objec-tives of the new regime. Its position on this point was legitimized by the pervasive, forward-looking nationalism that was part of the current development ideology. And finally, although the government's main strength was in the periphery, it was feared that failure to recognize the striking inequalities in the distribution of public investments and the resulting hiatus in levels of welfare and rates of growth, would lead to social tensions that might undermine the processes of national development itself. The periphery had supported the democratic revolution. Unless its economic position were strengthened, unless the center-periphery structure itself were broken down into a multicentric regional system, the periphery might shift its allegiance to those nondemocratic forces that claimed to be the bearers of a truly new order. After 1961 a major part of terrorist strength was operating from secret positions in the provinces. The memory of Fidel Castro roaming the Sierra Maestre was still vivid.

Intellectually, the regional issue assumed a somewhat complicated form. On the one hand, there was the overriding goal of national economic development with its implied purpose of creating a multicentric, interregional economy. But in regard to more concrete matters, this unambiguous sense of direction was quickly lost. First, there was the problem of balanced regional versus concentrated growth: for to disperse resources indiscriminately to the periphery would have meant to apply a sharp brake to the pace of national economic growth. Second, there was the problem of centralization versus decentralization in political power. The issue of regional planning was fought partly over how much effective decision power should be devolved to the states and municipalities. The traditional influence of Caracas was questioned.

EXPERIMENT AND DEMONSTRATION

Two experiences contributed to dramatize regional development planning in Venezuela: the Guayana program and Valencia. Although totally dissimilar in approach, both exerted a powerful demonstration effect on the rest of the country.

The Guayana program continues to be Venezuela's most ambitious bid at regional development. Located in the southeastern part of the country, more precisely, at the confluence of the Orinoco and Caroní Rivers, it amounted to a massive effort by the government to transform an ephemeral resource frontier into a major center of heavy industry. The Venezuelan Guayana Corporation (CVG) was created late in 1960 to take charge of all related developments in the area, including construction of a system of hydroelectric installations on the Caroní, the completion, operation, and expansion of a steel plant using local iron ores and the building of a new city around a core of basic industries. The corporation was vested with the extensive powers of an independent authority directly responsible to the presidency. Its main geographic area of activity was narrowly circumscribed as a development zone, but its effective powers extended beyond it whenever a functional relation to works within the zone could be demonstrated.[4]

This ambitious undertaking satisfied a deep national urge: the local influence of foreign mining corporations was broken; the steel mill symbolized the country's efforts at industrialization and the consequent liberation from an exclusive dependency on oil—a result which had political implications as well; and the new city of Santo Tomé de Guayana was seen as a significant opportunity for shifting population from the coast into the interior where the "true" Venezuela, it was believed, would be discovered. As a result of these potential effects, and because the program itself was carried on quietly and without public scandal, and also because it delivered a major World Bank loan for the construction of Guri Dam, it was rarely the subject of open criticism. Its physical achievements, on the other hand, were widely publicized.[5]

Prior to development work in the region, Guayana had been a relatively isolated, unpopulated area. It is, therefore, not unreasonable that other regions, more densely settled, should have found their own needs neglected. The CVG was looked upon as an appropriate model for obtaining the requisite resources for regional development. According to a widely held view, the solution of Venezuela's regional problem lay in the creation of additional regional development corporations or authorities. Although the CVG was physically located in Caracas rather than in Guayana itself, other corporations might easily be brought under the direct influence of regional interests.

The first concrete result of this new regionalist movement was the creation, by presidential decree, of the Andean Development Commission (Comisión Promotora del Desarollo de los Andes) on

January 8, 1962.[6] The commission was conceived as only a transitional agency, and it was charged with recommending a permanent successor. It was not unexpected, therefore, when the commission proposed its transformation into an Andean Development Corporation, on the model of the CVG.

The Andean commission had been the outgrowth of local initiative. According to its first comprehensive report, it owed its origin to "the preoccupation of a group of intellectuals and politicians from Táchira." [7] The president was requested to create some kind of regional development organization. Sympathetic reply from Caracas had "an extraordinary resonance throughout the entire region. Immediately Committees for the Creation of an Andean Development Corporation were set up in the state capitals of Trujillo, Mérida, and Táchira." [8] Quickly gathering momentum, the movement culminated in a regional conference in August 1961. Only four months later the Andean commission formally came into being.

The regional development program of the Andes was to be integrated with the national plan. But this proviso in the decree was more an expression of pious hope than realistic expectation. No institutional mechanism was created by which regional planning might be effectively coordinated with the national program.

That same year a similar grass roots effort to create a regional development authority was carried forward in the eastern provinces. The results, however, were inconclusive. CORDIPLAN was becoming seriously concerned with losing control over regional planning and with too great a dispersal of investment resources over the national territory. The proliferation of regional development agencies, it was thought, would lead to problems in the future because "the majority of these organisms do not maintain the necessary coördination with national efforts." [9] For the time being the proposal for an Eastern Development Corporation was shelved.

Valencia was an altogether different story. Situated at the center of a fertile intermontane basin, the city was only two hours from Caracas by car. During the 1950's, it had attracted a number of light import-substitution industries and was on the way to becoming a serious rival to the national capital as a center of manufacturing.

Its meteoric rise to prominence was due, in large measure, to the enterprising spirit of its leading citizens, acting through the Municipal Council. Not only were Valencians eminently successful in promoting their city as a good place for industry, they also invested substantial amounts of their own money in a well-planned industrial estate. In 1962 a private development foundation was chartered, in part to arrange for a foreign loan to underwrite the further development of the municipality. On the strength of this loan a contract was signed with a French firm of consultants to study the problems of future expansion of the city and to recommend basic policies and programs for action. The final report, the most comprehensive socioeconomic and urban planning survey for any city in Venezuela, was published in 1963.[10]

The remarkable success of the Valencia program has been widely admired. Although doubts have been expressed as to whether other municipalities would be able to follow suit, more and more cities have, in fact, been copying at least the material aspects of the program. A number of cities have built industrial estates similar to Valencia's, and others are to follow suit. As a result of Valencia's experience there is now a growing awareness that industrial development is an essentially competitive business in which communities must outbid each other in their efforts to attract private capital.

This arousal of civic spirit on the country's periphery gave further support to broader regional efforts at development. The Ministry of Development announced that it would sponsor a meeting of localities in the central region, from Tejerías to Morón, for the purpose of improving coordination of industrial development efforts.[11] If it should succeed, intermunicipal, interstate cooperation of the kind envisioned by the ministry would be a major innovation in Venezuelan politics. That such a proposal should have been made at all reflects a growing recognition that the power to make effective decisions about economic developments is slipping out of the hands of the central government into a more diffused sociopolitical structure. It is interesting to observe that the ministry should have spoken only of improved "coordination" rather than of imposing a definite program upon the area. It is likewise significant that the proposal came from an administrative body other than CORDIPLAN itself. Without ever having passed through the stage of a centrally planned economy, Venezuela appeared to be evolving toward a planning system in which more and more decisions would be made on the basis of planning principles within a loose coordinative framework that would depend more on dialogue among decision-makers than on explicit command.

But Guayana and Valencia were by no means the only programs that drew attention to the regional issue. A brief account of other activities will complete the picture.

To promote the policy of decentralization of the Venezuelan Development Corporation (CVF),

> five regional industrial Development Committees were established from April through October of 1961. These committees, set up in the states of Zulia, Falcón, Lara, Anzoátegui, and Monagas, seek to create an awareness of the importance of industrialization through a complete information program and the stimulation of regional efforts to found new industry. . . . In this program, the regional committees act as liaison agents between local groups and individuals and official agencies whose assistance is necessary. They also provide or secure technical assistance when needed. The committees are made up of representatives of the economic life of the region, designated by the CVF, plus a CVF regional official who acts as executive secretary of the committee.[12]

Additional committees were reported under study.

During the summer of 1962, Pro-Venezuela conducted a series of regional conferences throughout the country for the purpose of stimulating interest in the subject of regional development, and particularly in the development of manufacturing industries. The meetings were apparently gratifying to the participants and had wide publicity in the national press. Many specific proposals, including one for a Development Corporation for the Eastern Provinces, were made and submitted to the government.

The Agriculture Ministry has conducted, through the services of an international consulting consortium, a regional economic study of the state of Lara and surrounding areas focused on the city of Barquisimeto. A preliminary report of this study has been published, and efforts are currently under way to conduct a similar survey in eastern Venezuela.[13]

The Ministry of Public Works has established a Division of Regional Planning to assist in the coordination of its far-flung programs. A number of regional administrative offices have been set up.

In the fall of 1962 the first Latin American Conference on Regional Science was sponsored by the Center for Economic Development Studies (CENDES) of the Central University in Caracas. The conference devoted a good deal of its time to problems of regional development on the continent. It was not only widely attended, but the major papers presented were published and circulated in a Spanish edition.[14] The meeting reflected the growing interest in the subject; it also helped focus the attention of wider segments of the public on the regional problem.

The regional theme has been repeatedly stressed during the annual governors' conferences. At the most recent event, in 1963, the chief executives were arguing specifically for more effective administrative power at the state level. Among the proposals was one for the creation of "little CORDIPLANS" at the state level, together with a plea for better regional-national coordination in project formulation and implementation.[15]

In its election platform for 1963, the Democratic Action party stressed the importance of regional planning "for the purpose of accelerating the process of development of the more backward areas and to obtain a better utilization of local resources." [16] The need for continued efforts at "decentralization" and for creating sustained regional development was also emphasized.

A number of state planning commissions have been created during the past several years on the initiative of local governors. Although wanting in effectiveness, in view of the small amount of resources at the disposal of the states, these commissions have assisted their governments in gaining a more comprehensive overview of local economic problems and opportunities. Among the better-known commissions of this type are those in Bolívar, Anzoátegui, and Táchira.

Whether or not regional development represented the "new doctrine" of Venezuela's economic development, as it was on one occasion called, it certainly was much in the public eye, especially after 1960. And it has by no means spent its gathering momentum.

IN SEARCH OF A SOLUTION

The movement had been touched off by national planning efforts, somewhat contrary to the wishes of CORDIPLAN. But, confronted with the facts, CORDIPLAN found itself obliged to take a stand.

In the original planning legislation, the concept of regional planning had been mentioned as part of a national planning system. In principle, therefore, CORDIPLAN favored the decentralization of decision-making. But in actuality its point of view was ambiguous. Objections to regional planning were raised on a number of grounds. First, CORDIPLAN itself claimed no particular competence in the subject. None of its own staff had been trained in problems of regional development, and precise investment criteria were lacking. Second, the shortage of experts in regional development was advanced as a major argument against the extension of planning below the national level. Third, it was feared that regional planning would strengthen the bargaining position of local areas while reducing the ability of CORDIPLAN to assert its presumably more comprehensive, national point of view. In short, CORDIPLAN feared that the delicate balance between politics and planning that it had taken great pains to build up and maintain might be destroyed by rash adventures into regional planning. Finally, CORDIPLAN was aware of the political implications of any move toward decentralization in decision-making in the sense that this would eventually lead to a revitalization of regional politics and a general strengthening of the periphery's decision power over that of the center. And this, strictly speaking, was a matter lying outside its sphere of responsibility.

Subject to intensive pressures for regional development, however, CORDIPLAN could not simply remain a passive and essentially critical observer. After 1962 the agency slowly developed a positive point of view. An entire section in the national plan was devoted to a discussion of regional development planning. Two contradictory allocation criteria were proposed in it. According to the first, priority in investments should go to the more backward regions in the country; here equity was the main consideration. According to the second, priority should be given to those regions that promised the highest returns on investment, that is to say, the more advanced regions in the country; here economic growth was the main consideration.[17] Unable to decide between them, CORDIPLAN was left with no objective criterion at all. Is was, therefore, for the political process to decide on the best regional allocation of investment funds.

But more important than investment criteria was the organizational question. For this would have a direct bearing on how decisions would be made and on the important problem of coordination. Tentative and somewhat confusing steps were taken by the establishment of regional planning divisions within both CORDIPLAN and the Ministry of Public Works. Neither of these was adequately staffed or had a clear conception of its purposes.

In July 1963 CORDIPLAN helped establish the Zulia Planning Council as a possible model for future regional planning organizations. The administrative scheme of the council is interesting and essentially in line with the basic planning philosophy CORDIPLAN had been trying to promote. Represented on its board of directors (Conselho Directivo) are all principal interests active in the state, including government, military, church, business, industry, labor, and farmers. The five-man executive committee is headed by the governor of the state and serviced by a technical secretariat headed by CORDIPLAN technicians. Key to the organization, however, are its working groups, which concern themselves with specialized problems in agriculture, industry, public works, and services, and whose membership includes government officials as well as interested representatives from the private sector. Coordination with national planning would be achieved principally through the agency of the secretariat.

The council has its offices in Maracaibo, the state capital, and its area of competence includes primarily the State of Zulia. Its establishment had been urged on the government by local civic groups. If successful it would reproduce at the state level what CORDIPLAN has been trying to do at the national level. Private interests would join the government in a corporate endeavor at developmental planning. The political process would be improved by a more rational assessment of development possibilities and presenting investment projects for consideration at the national level in a more professional manner than had been the custom. Emotional regionalism, especially prevalent in Zulia, might thus be transformed into a more functional, objective attitude and, through CORDIPLAN representation on the secretariat, some coordination with national planning efforts would in principle be assured. In accepting regional planning, therefore, Zulia concurred in the proposition that its own planning and development efforts should in some sense be subordinated to the national interest. Whether the Zulia Planning Council will actually work in this manner remains to be seen. But the intention, at least, is clear.[18]

CORDIPLAN appeared once more to be moving toward a middle ground where a continuing dialogue could be maintained. It was drifting from its earlier position which had opposed the regionalization of economic devlopment planning on grounds that decentralization would slow the rate of economic growth. It was also drawing away from the alternative proposal to establish for each major region a special independent development corporation. In place of these extreme and contradictory positions. CORDIPLAN was beginning to assert a form of regional planning that would establish a framework for local-national coordination in development planning and extend to the several regions of the country the principle of "corporate" planning somewhat along the lines of recent French experience.

What, in the larger context, is the significance of regional planning? Its extension to local units of decision-making is intimately connected with that complex process frequently referred to as nation-building, which is the ultimate aim of current strivings toward economic development. Its hidden purpose is therefore to assist in the full integration of the national territory, in an economic no less than a political sense. If CORDIPLAN's brand of regional planning should be successful in Zulia and, by extension, in other parts of the country where it may eventually be introduced, its contribution will have to be measured in four quite different ways. First, one would expect each region—and the nation as a whole—to make more rapid economic gains than would otherwise have been made. This follows not only from the manifest function of developmental planning but also from the fact that in transitional societies many resources remain inadequately employed. Second, one would look forward to improved coordination between the public and private sectors, so that private decisions would be rendered more responsive to the public interest at the same time that public decisions are made to take into account a wider range of private concerns. Third, one would look for a shift in state politics away from the traditional emphasis on personalities to more substantive issues of development. Fourth, one would hope for greater political stability as a condition of steady national development. This would result from a multiplication of regional decision poles and a fuller recognition of the claims of peripheral states for greater political participation in the shaping of national policies.

None of these consequences, it may be argued, will be achieved without some loss of functional rationality, if by this is meant an exclusively expert technical judgment regarding the optimal employment of available means. For the extension of planning to regions will almost certainly render it subject to a wide range of political considerations. But, in a national view, the net-balance should probably be judged a gain. Dynamic political behavior is generally a sign that truly vital issues are at stake. The institutionalization of regional planning at the local level as a process in which politics is linked to objective decision functions will stimulate local concern with questions of development while emphasizing the realistic constraints that flow from increased knowledge and a growing awareness of strategic interdependencies at all levels. The presumed loss of functional rationality is probably a deception on the part of technicians who regard planning as an abstract process of maximizing goal achievement along a single dimension. But if economic development is viewed in the broader context of nation-making, the conclusion is inescapable that a strengthening of decision poles in the several regions of the country is a necessary condition for attaining the ultimate purposes of society.

The phenomenon of regional planning in this sense is temporary. Once a more nearly complete politicoeconomic integration across the national territory is achieved, once each major region has evolved an indigenous and healthy political life, regional planning is likely to disappear in its present form. But for at least a generation it will perform a significant role in the building of Venezuela as a prosperous and democratic nation.

V

The Future of National Planning

The preceding analysis of national planning in Venezuela was written in a perspective of hope, only a few weeks prior to the general elections which were held in December 1963. Their outcome has confirmed the early optimism. The transition to the new government was accomplished peacefully. Raúl Leoni, the candidate of Democratic Action as the government party, won by a plurality, followed by Rafael Caldera, candidate of the Christian Democrats (COPEI). Terrorism has declined. There is consequently reason for hoping that democratic institutions have taken a more secure hold and that progress will be made in advancing toward the ambitious goals that have been set. Assuming this will be the case, assuming that the middle class revolution will be carried forward without major interruption, let us speculate on what planning will be like ten or twenty years from now. In short, how will planning be changed under conditions or rapid economic development?

A distant time horizon is necessary for prognosis. The long-term future is easier to predict than specific events next year. By looking far ahead, some of the detail will be blurred, but major patterns will often be more clearly seen.

A few basic assumptions for the future of Venezuela must be granted: continued political stability; continued adherence to major developmental goals; continued rapid expansion of the gross national product; continued rapid industrialization; continued rapid urbanization; continued rapid demographic growth. Some of these parameters may be stated quantitatively, if only to give an idea of the implied magnitudes of change. Thus, the time necessary for a doubling of the gross national product may be assumed to be roughly ten years; of industrial output, six to seven years; of urban population, fifteen to eighteen years; and of total population, twenty-two to twenty-five years.

Four main vectors of change may be derived from these assumptions. They will form the basis for our exercise in prediction and include: progress toward a stable development society; shift from economic growth to welfare objectives; attenuation in the crisis of frustration; and increasing organizational complexity, growth in knowledge and communication, and progressive integration of the national economy.

Clearly, these vectors describe different, if closely related, aspects of the same pervasive movement of social change. The consequences they may be expected to have for national planning will to some degree overlap. Several of the vectors may influence planning in approximately the same way, providing reinforcement for changes already under way. This is an inescapable feature of the model we propose to use.

Progress toward a stable development society

A development society is one which regards its economic and political development in the sense of an increase in wealth and welfare and the modernization of political institutions as the major "project" of the living generation. Such a society came into being in Venezuela in 1958. After five years of democratic rule, it has begun to consolidate. To the extent to which its dominant ideology becomes progressively internalized by the population and provides the main motives for social and, to some extent, for individual behavior, the following consequences can be expected for planning.

The marginal significance of some of the identified latent functions of national planning will decline. Planning will no longer be widely supported because it tends to make political behavior more "responsible," or promotes a development society, or reduces social conflict, or aids in the mobilization of external resources. Much of the success of national planning during the past half-decade may be ascribed to these largely social implications. In the future some of these consequences may be no longer regarded as significant criteria for judging the performance of national planning.

As a corollary of this proposition, we should expect to find growing importance attached to the manifest functions of planning, to its achievements in promoting economic development, for example. This attitude will shift attention more to the technical repertory of planning. It will also place planners under increasing stress, since goal-attainment is a measurable function readily understood by the public. Under pressure to make goals coincide with the actual performance of the economy, planners will tend to become conservative in their setting of production and similar targets. The difference between "plan" and "forecast" will tend to be blurred.

As a result of the foregoing changes, planning will be regarded in a more matter-of-fact, utilitarian manner. It will be judged critically, and be treated increasingly as a tool which, if it fails to serve, will either be replaced or reshaped. As a result, frequent organizational changes of the planning function are likely to be attempted.

Shift from economic growth to welfare objectives

As over-all growth rates in production are achieved, questions of distribution will gain in relative importance. One of the major questions facing government will be how to redistribute the national income to achieve social welfare objectives. Since economic development over the next generation is not likely to eliminate differences in real income either among the population as a whole or among regions, and in some cases may even aggravate existing inequalities, the budget will come to be used increasingly as an instrumentality for effecting appropriate income transfers. This practice will raise certain difficulties for national planning, and lead to a reevaluation of its purposes, as follows:

1. Questions of redistribution and social investment are largely "qualitative" in the sense that objective criteria do not exist by which the optimality of a decision may be judged. Accordingly, expert planners will be little better qualified than other people in deciding on the allocation of an increasing amount of total government income. The planners' authority in these matters will be challenged, and political considerations will more often than not be invoked.

2. The scope of technical planning will consequently become restricted to a relatively small number of quantifiable objectives

where means and ends can be better evaluated in relation, and where the ends themselves are not seriously questioned. Planning will become increasingly concerned, then, with such problems as maintaining an adequate growth rate for the economy under conditions of stability, achieving full employment, and maintaining a favorable balance of payments. Planners are likely to withdraw from involvement in issues where their expertness is put in doubt.

Attenuation in the crisis of frustration

As progress is made throughout the economy, and the grossest inequalities in welfare are diminished, and especially as the possibility of successful upward mobility is put within reach of larger segments of the population, the current deep sense of dissatisfaction with the existing order is likely to become less critical. In the long run, the level of consumption may become more significant as a measure of the economy's health than investment. Growth itself will increasingly become demand-induced. These changes will affect planning in a number of ways.

The urgency for investment planning will decline, and adequate political support for continuing effective investment planning may, therefore, fail to be forthcoming in the same measure as before.

As government resorts increasingly to "traditional" measures of fiscal-monetary policy, the center of gravity in national planning may shift from an institution such as CORDIPLAN to the Central Bank, the Ministry of Finance, and groups of special government advisors.

As the crisis of frustration becomes attenuated, investment planning is likely to give greater emphasis than now to long-term studies and thus to shift from an essentially tactical to a strategic approach. Since politics is chiefly interested in the immediate impact of action, however, the investment planners will more and more move into rarefied regions of econometric models where politics do not intrude. As a consequence, the technical quality of investment planning is likely to be much improved, but its effectiveness diminished. To the extent to which planning stresses the long view and is isolated from the political currents that move the country, its ability to influence actual decisions will be reduced.

Increasing organizational complexity; growth in knowledge and communication; progressive integration of the national economy

These terms belong together. They are characteristic of all structural growth. Increasing complexity refers here specifically to an increase in the number of independent, or quasi-independent, decision units in society. And if this growing system is to be maintained, it must have a vastly increased volume of information inputs. Economic development itself, which leads to greater internal differentiation as suggested, also takes place through greater integration of economic activities across sectors and regions. Integration occurs sectorally chiefly through the extension of commodity, capital, and labor markets to the entire national territory, and spatially through a hierarchical national system of cities. As a result, national planning will be forced to undergo some major changes.

Decision-making will become increasingly fragmented and competitive. The ability to coordinate economic decisions through direct consultations will be progressively reduced. Even a minimum working consensus may be hard to obtain. Although government can be expected to play an important role in economic decisions, to the extent to which government enterprise is involved, it will behave more nearly as private firms would, showing quite as much independence of public policies in the pursuit of maximizing profits or any other set of objectives internal to the enterprise itself.

With increasing multicentricity of the economic system, the need for a common framework of assumptions and information will be felt. National planning, therefore, will tend increasingly to concentrate on generating information that may be useful to lower-order decisions. Coordination will come to be viewed as a function chiefly of the right kind of information, which may include statements of government intentions, projections of basic variables, price forecasts, and other data relevant for economic decisions.

Direct manipulation will be given up in preference to indirect methods of system-wide control, preferably to those which operate automatically whenever selected performance indexes exceed or fall below optimal tolerances.

The changes foreseen for national planning, under the assumptions stated, are very substantial. Undoubtedly, some elements of present-day planning will be retained in some form, for instance, the new methods for permanent consultations with the private sector. But in many other respects national planning in the 1970's and 1980's will be altogether different from what is known today. It is suggested here that national planning in Venezuela will eventually bear a strong resemblance to national planning in advanced non-communist countries today. What is therefore likely to occur is a decline in the central function of planning, but also a concurrent increase of rationality among a multiplicity of decision units related to each other in a loosely coordinated information-decision system. Fragmentation of decision units also implies interdependency, however, so that even relatively simple decisions must be made by taking into account the effects of decision units on each other. That is but another way of saying that decisions become inevitably more responsible. The traditional distinction between private and public is already disappearing in Venezuela and may become altogether inappropriate in the future. If this should happen, as it is bound to if experience in the United States and Europe is any indication, some independence of action will no doubt be lost. But in compensation there will emerge a society in which planning as comprehensive foresight, instrumental rationality, and, in more general terms, as purposive behavior will have become the normal mode of organizational action. The members of this society will be finely attuned to each other and to the requirements of the system to which they belong and will be bound in their decisions by an interlocking hierarchy of constraints operating to assure the satisfactory performance of the system as a whole.

Notes to Chapters

I. BACKGROUND

1. Raúl Leoni, Jóvito Villalba, Raúl Ramos Giménez, Arturo Uslar Pietri, Rafael Caldera, Wolfgang Larrazábal, and Juan German Borregales.

2. *V. Mensaje Presidencial* (Caracas: Miraflores, March 12, 1963), p. 29.

3. Some basic reference works used in this study include: Edwin Lieuwen, *Venezuela* (London: Oxford University Press, 1961); *The Economic Development of Venezuela,* Published for The International Bank for Reconstruction and Development (Baltimore: Johns Hopkins Press, 1961); Carl S. Shoup, *The Fiscal System of Venezuela: A Report* (Baltimore: Johns Hopkins Press, 1959); Rodolfo Luzardo, *Notas Histórico-Económicas, 1928–1963* (Caracas: Ed. Sucre, 1963); Arturo Uslar Pietri, *Sumário de Economía Venezolana* (2nd ed., Caracas: Fundación Eugenio Mendoza, 1958); Banco Central de Venezuela, *Memória;* Oficina Central de Coordinación y Planificación, *Plan de la Nación, 1963–1966* (Caracas, May 1963).

4. A "conflict and consensus study" has been undertaken by the Center for Economic Development Studies (CENDES) of the Central University, in collaboration with the M.I.T. Center for International Studies. When completed, this study should throw much light on the patterns of social tension existing during the period covered by the present research.

5. An outstanding instance of recent history is the Peasant League Movement in Northeastern Brazil.

6. Chief spokesman for the neoliberals was Ramón Díaz, a steady contributor to two right-wing publications, *La Esfera* and *Observaciónes Económicas.* Ramón Díaz is responsible for the phrase "fomento de la miséria" in reference to Venezuela's "planned" economic development (*La Esfera,* March 19, 1963). He also acquired some notoriety in speaking of the Alliance for Progress as an "Alliance for Misery." Notable among the intellectually respectable Marxists is Professor D. F. Maza Zavala of the Central University. His favorite outlet as a publicist is the daily newspaper *Clarín.* Maza Zavala referred to national planning in Venezuela as a complete failure (*Clarín,* May 30, 1963) because it did

not provide for "basic structural changes" in the social economy of the country. For him the Alliance for Progress was nothing but a "multilateral pact of governments against revolutionary change." (*El Nacional,* February 20, 1963).

7. A revealing insight is provided in an article written by Wolfgang Larrazábal in the respected Caracas newspaper, *El Nacional* (July 19, 1963). Larrazábal had presided for several months over the provisional government in 1958. Five years later, he was running as an independent candidate for the presidency. In the article referred to, he saw it necessary to defend his position on national planning in view of the Emergency Plan which his government had promulgated in 1958. The Emergency Plan had been simply a stop-gap, make-work program to alleviate catastrophic unemployment immediately after the overthrow of the dictatorship. The program had been sharply criticized for its lack of "real" planning. Larrazábal now wished to be put on record that he, like his critics, was in favor of "planning" and that the improvisations of 1958, though necessary then, do not reflect his basic thinking on how economic development programs should, in principle, be conceived.

II. THE ORIGINS OF PLANNING

1. Tejera Paris had been, variously, student leader, professor of economics and public adminstration at the Central University, member of the staff of the United Nations, public administrator, member of the board of directors of the Federation of Chambers of Commerce and Industry, political activist in the Democratic Action party, Governor of Sucre, and Ambassador to the United States.

2. Decree No. 492. The Commission Report has been published under the title, *Sistema Nacional de Coordinación y Planificación. Informe Presentado a la Junta de Gobierno de la República de Venezuela por la Comisión Preparatoria del Sistema Nacional de Coordinación y Planificación Gubernmental* (2 vols.; Caracas, 1958).

3. Commission Report, p. xii.

4. Decree No. 492, Art. 2. This and all subsequent translations are by the writer.

5. *Ibid.,* Articles 3 and 4.

6. *Ibid.,* Art. 6.

7. *Ibid.,* Art. 7.

8. *Ibid.,* Art. 23.

9. *Ibid.,* Art. 12 (f).

10. *El Nacional,* June 23, 1963.

11. Although difficult to measure, the middle class in Venezuela was

definitely a minority group at the time. Some idea of its numerical strength may be got from the following statistics. At the time of the national census in 1961, only 14 per cent of the labor force was accounted for by typically middle class occupations, including professionals, technicians, managers, and office workers. Of these, 43 per cent were located in Caracas. Cf. Ministerio de Fomento, *Memória y Cuenta, 1962*, pp. 1039 and 1081. The university-educated elite is very much smaller than the figures above suggest, and probably includes no more than 2 per cent of the adult population, and quite possibly less.

12. Acción Democrática, *Acción Democrática. Doctrina y Programa* (1st ed.; Caracas: Secretaria de Propaganda, 1962), pp. 57ff.

13. For a discussion of the role of these values in a context of economic transition, cf. John Friedmann, "Intellectuals in Developing Societies," *Kyklos, Vol.* XIII, No. 4 (1960), pp. 513–44.

14. *Declaración sobre aspectos fundamentales de la política económica* (Miraflores, May 30, 1962).

15. *Ibid.,* p. 3.

16. *V. Mensaje Presidencial,* p. 29.

17. Acción Democrática, especially pp. 227–28.

18. This image was promoted by the planners themselves. It departed from the neoliberal view of planning, which may be most succinctly described as "the control of free enterprise by the government."

19. This interpretation owes much to the brilliant speculations of Peter Wiles in his book, *The Political Economy of Communism* (Cambridge: Harvard University Press, 1963), Part IV. The relative expansion of a "classless segment" in the United States, already involving roughly half the population, has recently been noted. Cf. Kurt B. Meyer, "Does America Still Have Social Classes?" *Schweizerische Zeitschrift für Volkswirtschaft und Statistik.* Vol. 99, No. 2 (June 1963), 158–71 (in German).

20. Acción Democrática, p. 46.

21. A notable exception to this assertion is found in the writings of Karl Mannheim, particularly in *Man and Society in an Age of Reconstruction* (New York: Harcourt, Brace and Co., 1949). The German-language edition of this book appeared in Holland in 1935. But Mannheim was a sociologist and thought principally in terms of Western Europe, rather than Latin America, when he presented his ideas on democratic planning as "the third way" between communism and free enterprise capitalism. It is highly unlikely that his ideas were well known among the Venezuelan intelligentsia in 1939.

22. The following were among the outstanding early contributions: Harvey S. Perloff, *Puerto Rico's Economic Future* (Chicago: University

of Chicago Press, 1950); United Nations, *Measures for the Economic Development of Under-Developed Countries*. Report by a Group of Experts (New York, 1951); United Nations, Technical Assistance Administration, *Formulation and Economic Appraisal of Development Projects* (2 vols.; New York, 1951); Paul A. Baran, "On the Political Economy of Backwardness," *The Manchester School of Economic and Social Studies* (January 1952) pp. 66–84; S. H. Frankel, *The Economic Impact on Under-Developed Societies* (New York: Oxford University Press, 1953); Ragnar Nurkse, *Problems of Capital Formation in Underdeveloped Countries* (New York: Oxford University Press, 1953). Textbooks on economic development did not appear until 1955.

23. Alvin Cohen, "ECLA and the Economic Development of Peru," *Inter-American Economic Affairs*, XVII (Summer 1963), 3–28.

24. United Nations Economic Commission for Latin America, Servício de Información, "Hacía una Dinámica del Desarollo Latinoamericano" (April 1963), Mimeo.

25. United Nations, 1950.

26. United Nations Economic Commission for Latin America, "Preliminary Study of the Technique of Programming Economic Development." (Document E/CN.12/292); and United Nations, Department of Economic and Social Affairs, *Analysis and Projections of Economic Development*, I. An Introduction to the Technique of Programming (New York, 1955).

27. United Nations Economic Commission for Latin America, *Analysis and Projections*, p. 3.

28. José Antonio Mayobre, "Global Programming as an Instrument of Economic Development Policy," with comments by Eugenio Gudin and H. D. Higgins, in Howard S. Ellis, ed., *Economic Development for Latin America*. Proceedings of a Conference held by the International Economics Association (London: Macmillan, 1961), pp. 29–56.

29. Enrique Tejera Paris, *Dos Elementos de Gobierno* (Caracas: no publisher given, 1960), Pt. II, "La Administración Pública y la Política de Desarollo" (Informe a la Asemblea de la CEPAL, Mayo 1957).

30. *Ibid.*, p. 139.

31. An aspect of this genealogy of Venezuelan planning is of some interest. It was Rexford Tugwell who, as Governor of Puerto Rico during the Second World War, had established the legislative framework for planning in what was shortly to become the Commonwealth and had personally selected the individuals who would become the key figures in Puerto Rican planning. Tugwell went from his governorship to the University of Chicago, where he initiated one of the most exciting experiments in American planning education, the Program for Education

and Research in Planning. Luís Lander went on, in 1960, to help establish a planning school in Caracas, the Centro de Estudios del Desarollo (CENDES), which was closely patterned after the Chicago model. Tugwell's ideas on planning differed greatly from those of Enrique Tejera Paris. Still, this interweaving of causal relations is interesting as an example of the basic continuities in intellectual tradition. It might be added that the writer of this study is himself a product of Tugwell's planning school. Tugwell's writings on planning are widely scattered in the professional literature. A good summary of them, however, appears in his lectures, *The Place of Planning in Society*. Puerto Rico Planning Board, Technical Paper 7 (San Juan, 1954). An account of the Chicago Planning School is found in Harvey S. Perloff, *Education for Planning: City, State, and Regional*. Published for Resources for the Future (Baltimore: Johns Hopkins Press, 1957), Part III. CENDES is described in its Annual Report *(Informe Anual)* for 1962.

32. *Sistema Nacional de Coordinación y Planificación,* I, xiii.

33. The preceding discussion of the crisis of frustration and its effect on the acceptability of national planning is not grounded in extensive documentation. It is based primarily on more or less random comments by Venezuelans made to the writer during the summers of 1962 and 1963, as well as by a number of newspaper articles that have come to his attention. The earlier-mentioned "conflict and consensus study" (note 4 to Chapter I) will provide whatever evidence may be needed to prove or disprove the contention made.

34. This type of planning is beautifully illustrated in Ely Devon's study of wartime planning in Britain, *Planning in Practice* (Cambridge: Cambridge University Press, 1950).

35. In many South American countries national planning came to be instituted after the signing of the Punta del Este Declaration which created the Alliance for Progress. The Alliance, acting through the Committee of Nine, subsequently made the presentation of sound national plans virtually a condition of foreign aid. This proviso helped to *maintain* planning in Venezuela. But resource mobilization was not among the reasons which led to the establishment of a national planning system in that country. Cf. *V. Mensaje Presidencial* for a recognition of the Alliance's role in supporting national planning in Venezuela.

III. THE EVOLUTION OF PLANNING

1. *El Nacional,* June 29, 1963, p. C-2.

2. Quoted in Luis Fernando Yepez, "Fedecámeras y el Plan de la Nación," *El Nacional,* July 16, 1963, p. A-4.

3. In this the model of French national planning was apparently being followed. A number of descriptions of this model are now available. The most comprehensive of these is by John and Anne-Marie Hackett, *Economic Planning in France* (Cambridge: Harvard University Press, 1963).

4. By comparison the French planning staff is reported to number 140 employees, including drivers, office boys, and secretaries. Cf. Pierre Massé, "The Guiding Ideas Behind French Planning," in PEP, *Economic Planning in France,* Vol. XXVII, No. 454, August 14, 1961, p. 212.

5. Enrique Tejera Paris, *Dos Elementos,* p. 139.

6. Enrique Tejera Paris, "Planificación Nacional," in Universidad de Zulia, *Primer Cursillo de Planificación,* Maracaibo, April 1959, p. 31.

7. *Plan de la Nación, 1963–1966,* p. xii.

8. *El Nacional,* June 16, 1963.

9. Federación Venezolana de Cámeras y Asociaciones de Comercio y Producción, *Carta Económica de Mérida.* May–June 1962, p. 5.

10. Authors like Ludwig van Mises and Friedrich Hayek are repeatedly cited in such neoliberal publications as *La Esfera* and *Observaciónes Económicas.*

11. A good account of its activities is given in Asociación Pro-Venezuela, *Memória y Cuenta, 1961–1962.*

12. See Chapter IV of this study for further discussion of this point.

13. See especially pp. 24–25.

14. *El Nacional,* June 26, 1963, p. C-8.

15. *El Nacional,* July 14, 1963, p. C-12.

16. *El Nacional,* July 16, 1963, p. A-4.

17. A further indication of the oligarchy's collapse is the inability of AVI to agree to support a single candidate for the presidency of Venezuela. A conservative faction favored Arturo Uslar Pietri, an independent and greatly respected candidate, running on a national unity platform. After the elections internal disunity within AVI became more pronounced and contributed to a public image of impotence.

18. This terminology was first introduced by Robert Merton. Cf. his *Social Theory and Social Structure* (New York: Free Press, 1949), ch. 1.

19. Robert A. Dahl, "The Politics of Planning," *International Social Science Journal,* Vol. XI, No. 3 (1959), 340.

20. Yehezkel Dror, "The Planning Process: a Facet Design," *International Review of Administrative Sciences,* Vol. XXIX, No. 1 (1963), 5.

21. Sociedad Interamericana de Planificación, *La Enseñanza de*

la Planificación en la America Latina. San Juan, P.R., May–September 1960, p. 121.

22. *Ibid.,* p. 123.

23. *Ibid.*

24. Fred Levy, a graduate student in economics at Yale University and a lecturer at Syracuse University, is preparing his doctoral dissertation on economic decision-making in Venezuela. Conversations with Levy suggest that considerable evidence exists in support of the assertion made.

25. For instance, Martin Meyerson and Edward C. Banfield, *Politics, Planning, and the Public Interest.* The Case of Public Housing in Chicago (New York: Free Press, 1955); Edward C. Banfield, *Political Influence* (New York: Free Press, 1961); W. H. Brown, Jr., and C. E. Gilbert, *Planning Municipal Investment.* A Case Study of Philadelphia. (Philadelphia: University of Pennsylvania Press, 1961); and Ely Devon, *Planning in Practice* (Cambridge: Cambridge University Press, 1950).

26. This story was told to the writer by a high government official.

27. *New York Times,* November 3, 1963, p. 36, col. 1.

28. This point was made explicitly by Luis Vallenilla, President of the Venezuelan Development Corporation, in a speech to the Venezuelan Association of Executives. *El Nacional,* July 21, 1963, p. D-1.

29. *V. Mensaje Presidencial,* p. 29.

30. *The Economic Development of Venezuela* (IBRD), ch. 12.

31. The concept of rationality as such may not, of course, have a great deal of persuasive power. What is meant here are statements such as the following, with which Luís Lander opened the first planning course in Venezuela, at the University of Zulia, in March 1959:

> Planning is known today as the process of ordering and forecasting in order to obtain, through the establishment of objectives and by means of rational action, the optimal utilization of resources of a society at a certain period of its evolution. . . . Planning is, therefore, also a process which consists of the totality of measures by means of which politicians, technicians, and public administrators set into motion and maintain a process in order to meet the proposed objectives. (Universidad de Zulia, *Primer,* p. 9.)

Planning could be sold as an efficient means for goal achievement. Essentially philosophical concepts, such as "rationality," "optimality," and "social welfare," were generally introduced only elliptically to make planning sound all the more imposing.

IV. CREATING A DEVELOPMENT SOCIETY

1. For a detailed analysis of the evolution of a center-periphery structure in Venezuela, cf. John Friedmann, "El crecimiento económico y la estructura urbana de Venezuela," *Revista de Economia Latinoamericana,* No. 6 (1962), pp. 115–204. A fuller account is given in a forthcoming book by the author, *Regional Development Policy* (Cambridge: M.I.T. Press, 1965).

2. Public Administration Service, *Relations of Nation, States, and Municipalities in the Government of the Republic of Venezuela.* (Chicago, 1959). Cf. also Shoup, *Fiscal System,* ch. XII. According to the Shoup Mission Report (p. 313), "The bulk of government spending, and hence decisions over the allocation of public funds is in the hands of the national government. The national government also provides, through the constitutional and supporting grants, about 90 per cent of the revenues of the states and territorial governments."

3. The period of democratic government in 1948 was too short to have had any significant impact on the distribution of effective political power.

4. Decree No. 430, December 29, 1960.

5. Cf. Corporación Venezolana de Guayana, *Memória 1962.*

6. Decree No. 675, January 8, 1962.

7. Comisión Promotora del Desarollo de los Andes, *Primer Enfoque del Diagnóstico Económico de la Region de los Andes y sus Zonas de Influencia.* (Mérida, 1963), p. 1, Mimeo.

8. *Ibid.*

9. *El Nacional,* July 11, 1963, p. C-10.

10. Consejo Municipal de Valencia, *Plan de Crecimiento del Distrito Valencia* (Caracas: Ed. Arte, 1963).

11. *El Nacional,* July 14, 1963, p. C-4.

12. Corporación Venezolana de Fomento, *Report 1960–61,* p. 60 (in English).

13. A summary of the report of the West-Central Region appears in *Plan de la Nación,* pp. 443–45.

14. *Revista de Economia Latinoamericana,* No. 6 (1962). Special number.

15. *El Nacional,* June 19, 1963, p. C-1.

16. *El Nacional,* July 4, 1963, p. C-1.

17. *Plan de la Nación,* p. 414.

18. For a discussion of the organizational problems of regional planning in Venezuela, cf. *ibid.,* pp. 416–18.

Selected Bibliography

Acción Democrática. *Acción Democrática: Doctrina y Programa.* 1st ed., Caracas: Secretaria de Propaganda, 1962.

Ahumada, Jorge. "La Planificación del Desarollo," *Cuadernos de la Sociedad Venezolana de Planificación.* Vol. 1, No. 1, August 1962, pp. 1–23.

Betancourt, Rómulo. *Venezuela: Política y Petróleo.* Mexico: Fondo de Cultura Económico, 1956.

The Economic Development of Venezuela. Published for the International Bank for Reconstruction and Development. Baltimore: Johns Hopkins Press, 1961.

Ellis, Howard S., ed. *Economic Development for Latin America.* London: Macmillan, 1961.

Federación Venezolana de Cámeras y Asociaciones de Comércio y Producción. *Carta Económica de Merida.* May–June 1962.

Friedmann, John. *Regional Development Policy: A Case Study of Venezuela.* Cambridge: M.I.T. Press, 1965.

Johnson, John J. *Continuity and Change in Latin America.* Stanford: Stanford University Press, 1964.

———. *Political Change in Latin America: The Emergence of the Middle Sectors.* Stanford: Stanford University Press, 1958.

Levy, Fred, Jr. "National Economic Planning in Venezuela." Unpublished Ph.D. dissertation, Department of Economics, Yale University, 1965.

Lieuwen, Edwin. *Arms and Politics in Latin America.* Rev. ed. New York: Praeger, 1961.

———. *Venezuela.* London: Oxford University Press, 1961.

Luzardo, Rodolfo. *Notas Histórica-Económicas, 1928–1963.* Caracas: Ed. Sucre, 1963.

Moreno, A. Arellano. *Origenes de la Economía Venezolana.* 2nd ed. Caracas-Madrid: Edime, 1960.

Oficina Central de Coordinación y Planificación. *Plan de la Nación, 1963–1966.* Caracas, 1963.

Shoup, Carl S. *The Fiscal System of Venezuela: A Report.* Baltimore: Johns Hopkins Press, 1959.

Tejera Paris, Enrique. *Dos Elementos de Gobierno.* Caracas: no publisher given, 1960.

Tinbergen, Jan. *Central Planning*. New Haven and London: Yale University Press, 1964.

United Nations. "Progress in Planning in Latin America," *Economic Bulletin for Latin America*. Vol. VIII, No. 2, October 1963, pp. 129–46.

————. *Towards a Dynamic Development Policy for Latin America*. New York, 1963.

Index

AD (Democratic Action Party): 6, 8, 9, 12, 22, 24, 35, 42, 43, 50, 64, 69
Agriculture Ministry: 63
Alliance for Progress: 23, 54
Amazon River area: 4
American Military Mission: 1
Americans for Democratic Action: 42
Andean Development Commission. *See* CPDA
Angarita, Medina (Gen.): 6
Anzoátegui: 43, 63, 64
Aragua: 43
Armed Forces of Cooperation. *See* FAC
Armed Forces of National Liberation. *See* FALN
Association of Economics: 32
AVI (Independent Venezuelan Association): 42, 43
Axis: 6

Barcelona: 3, 9, 45, 46
Barquisimeto: 63
Betancourt, Rómulo (Pres.): 2, 6, 8, 10, 14, 26, 35, 44, 46, 56
Brazil: 55
Budget Council: 15

Caldera, Rafael: 69
Carabobo: 43
Caracas: size, 4, 5, 6; citizen uprising, 8; lack of regional balance, 12; CORDIPLAN location, 34; mentioned, 42, 43, 50, 54, 58, 59, 60, 61, 64
Caribbean: 4
Caroní River: 59, 60
Carúpano: 9
Castro, Fidel: 59

Castro Leoni (Gen.): 44
CENDES (Center for Economic Development Studies): 63
Central Bank: 15, 52, 72
Central Office of Coordination and Planning. *See* CORDIPLAN
Central University: 64
Chambers of Commerce and Industry. *See* Fedecámeras
Chile: 41
Christian Democrats. *See* COPEI
Ciudad Bolívar: 51, 64
Communism: 1, 2, 9, 19, 23, 24, 27, 38, 40, 44, 54
Communist Party of Venezuela. *See* PCV
Conservatives: 12, 43
COPEI (Christian Democrats): 69
CORDIPLAN (Central Office of Coordination and Planning): 15–17, 30–40, 45, 49–53, 62, 64, 65, 66, 72
Council of Ministers: 16
CPDA (Andean Development Commission): 60, 61
Cuba: 10
CVF (Venezuelan Development Corporation): 45, 63
CVG (Venezuelan Guayana Corporation): 60, 61

Democratic Action party. *See* AD
Democratic party: 19
Development Corporation for the Eastern Provinces: 63
"Día de Estudiantes" (1928): 6
Diagnosis of the National Economy: 40
Division of Regional Planning: 63

ECLA (United Nations Economic Commission for Latin America): 24, 25, 26, 36, 41

85

National Planning Series

BERTRAM M. GROSS, *General Editor*

The contributors to this unique series analyze national economic planning in a variety of pre-industrial, industrial, and "post-industrial" societies. Coming from many different disciplines and countries, the authors have produced fact-based studies of people and groups struggling with the difficulties of plan implementation as well as formulation. They present a variety of viewpoints—political, sociological, managerial, historical, and psychological, as well as economic.

Together, they provide a broad picture of the complexities of guided social change in the modern world. Future volumes will consider economic development and growth in Israel, Italy, West Germany, Britain, the Soviet Union, France, and other nations.

1 Venezuela: *From Doctrine to Dialogue*
JOHN FRIEDMANN

This volume studies in depth the work of CORDIPLAN, Venezuela's national planning organization, recognized as the outstanding example of democratic planning in Latin America. It also explores a number of unusual theoretical propositions about planning. $2.95

2 Morocco-Tunisia: *Politics and Planning*
DOUGLAS ELLIOTT ASHFORD

Professor Ashford analyzes the differences in the political and social climate of these two North African countries in an effort to explain why one country (Tunisia) is succeeding and the other (Morocco) is failing at planning efforts. $2.75

3 Tanganyika: *Preplanning*
FRED G. BURKE

Written from a historical viewpoint, this study of planning in Tanganyika points out the relevance of Tanganyikan plan formulation and implementation for the new state of Tanzania. $3.25

4 Mexico: *Mutual Adjustment Planning*
ROBERT J. SHAFER

This first large-scale examination of Mexican national economic development planning emphasizes particularly its sectoral and regional nature in the light of local environment and aspirations. $4.25

at your bookseller or
Syracuse University Press • Syracuse, New York 13210